MW01531681

Roots of a Christian Family

All Scripture taken from *The Holy Bible: King James Version.* 1995 (electronic ed. of the 1769 edition of the 1611 Authorized Version.). Bellingham WA: Logos Research Systems, Inc. Used by permission. All rights reserved.

ISBN 13: 978-0-615-90674-4

Transcriptions: Stephen C. Allen, Wendy Cass
Editor-In-Chief: William J. Clark, Jr.
Editing: Nancy C. Allen, Stephen C. Allen
Photographs: The Allen Family
Interior Design: William J. Clark, Jr.
Front Cover Design: Stephen C. Allen, Practical Photography & Publishing
Back Cover Design: David W. Allen, Stephen C. Allen

Printed in the United States of America
U.S. Printing History
November 2013 – HWA Ink

HWA Ink, Inc. POB 502568, Indianapolis, IN 46250

Dedicated to Dr. Harold Allen
on his 80th birthday!

As the sons of Dr. Harold Allen,
we can both honestly say that there was
never "one thing" that our parents did right.
It was a lifestyle built on the foundation
of Christian faith. No matter how badly
we messed up, their "net" was always there
to catch us and allow us another chance.

Because of this, we had the freedom
to walk out on limbs that might break,
with no fear of falling or failing. We truly
had parents who let us succeed.

TABLE OF CONTENTS

FOREWORD

Mom and dad love us. There were days when we questioned their reasons and decisions, but we have never questioned their love for us.

This book contains a series of messages that dad preached over the years. They are transcribed from Sunday morning church service tapes (yes, cassette tapes) and were selected for their timeless wisdom on parenting. Dad has always preached LOVE. That is why these chapters are more than sermons. They are love letters; words given to dad by a loving God. Words passed on to parents who, like mom and dad, love their children so very much. They speak of responsibilities, challenges and personal experiences. They are spoken with a gentle spirit.

As children grow they make memories. We have many. There was the night when I was babysitting Stephen. After being taunted by a younger brother, I chased Stephen through the house throwing oranges at him. When dad came home to find the orange pulp and juice on the living room walls, his belt found our backsides. Then, there was the day we helped dad in the yard. As the day came to an end, dad made popcorn, poured it in a paper bag and took us to the drive-in to see "Willy Wonka and the Chocolate Factory."

There was the Wednesday evening at church when I got into a fight in the fellowship hall. Dad ripped the "Harold W. Allen, Pastor" sign off his door and spanked me right there in the church office. We also remember many nights being pulled around the lake in a rubber raft, so we could catch bullfrogs. One night Stephen fell out of a tree at 11 pm. Dad was there as the doctor placed casts on two broken arms.

You get the idea – dad parented. He loved us on the days when we loved him. He loved us through the tears of punishment. He loved us when we messed up and when we made him proud. He modeled God's love for us. Pastor Rob Bell once said, "There is nothing you can ever do to make me love you less." That's dad. His love is consistent and unconditional. Just like God's love for each of us.

God says to us, no matter where we are in life, "There is nothing you can ever do to make Me love you less." There will be days when we question God, get frustrated or angry with God, even wonder if

1

God cares. But, never ask the question, "Does God love me?" He does. Very much. With all of His heart.

As you read these love letters, may you be filled with the knowledge and wonder of God's love. May you feel the love Christ felt for you, His child, as He hung on a cross and said to the world, "There is nothing you can ever do to make Me love you less."

Dr. David W. Allen

Dr. Harold and Nancy Allen

INTRODUCTION

This book is about how to raise godly children. I approach this subject with a lot of humility and anxiety. I do not have all the answers. I am no expert. I made a lot of mistakes raising my children.

Before I had children, I had a simple sermon: "10 Rules for Raising Good Kids." I thought that if folks would follow these rules, I could guarantee they would have a good child. And then I had a son.

I changed my sermon to "Helpful Hints for Raising Children." Then, I had a second son.

And I changed my sermon to "Feeble Hints from a Fellow Struggling Parent." And during the teen years, I was strangely silent on the subject. I had no advice, at all!

Now, as a grandparent I can simply say, "Good luck parents! Do the best you can."

But, I think God has something to say to us on how to raise kids. I think the beginning of any series of sermons on raising children is simply about who we are going to listen to, the world or God? Where are we going to go for our advice and counsel: to the experts in the world, or to the Word of God?

Dr. Harold W. Allen

Dr. Harold W. Allen

CHAPTER 1: HOW TO HANDLE YOUR CHILDREN

First Baptist Church, Gallatin, Tennessee

<u>May 11, 1975</u>

I approach the subject of raising children with much humility, or at least anxiety, because I am a parent and I am very sensitive about the subject. I know someone is going to say, "If you are so hot about raising kids, then let's wait and see what kind of job you do. Then, if we approve, maybe you speak about it."

I realize that if one has raised a successful son or daughter, and even if one does not have a child, people often speak with authority on how to raise children. But, we all know that during those years when your children are growing up... those are silent years. You don't say very much about raising kids because you are afraid to do so. You are afraid you are going to have to eat your words! We, as parents, are threatened when someone says, "Show us! Let's see what you are going to do with your kids!" We get sensitive, and we clam up on the subject.

When I was a young, unmarried student pastor I had several wonderful sermons on how to raise children. It was very simple. I would tell the parents to bring their children to church and Sunday school, and then the children would grow up to be the pride in their parents' eye. But the years have gone by, and a lot of the "cock-sureness" has been knocked out of me. I have come to realize that there are no pat formulas for raising children. I have heard it said that if you play together and pray together, you will stay together. I have found out that that doesn't work all the time either. There are no simple formulas. There are no pat answers to raising children.

I have often said that before I had any children, I had a dozen good sermons about raising children. Then, David came along and I burnt up 6 of them. Then, Stephen came along and I destroyed the others. It left me without any sermons at all on raising children!

7

Dr. Harold W. Allen

REALIZE THAT EVERY CHILD IS UNIQUE

I have come to realize that every child is different. No two children are alike; no two children are raised in the same environment. No two children have the same hereditary. Thus, there is no pat formula that is the same for every child.

It is a very difficult thing being a parent, trying to raise each child as an individual, trying to understand your child, and trying to accept that what will work in one situation will not necessarily work in another. What will work with one child may not work with the other. Even though children may live in the same environment, they may have the same parents, they may have the same material things and be raised in the same church, and they can still go entirely different directions!

If I had any word of advice to parents today, I would simply say, first of all, accept your child as an individual. Do not try to make him a carbon copy of you because he is not a carbon copy. Let him be a child, and let him grow up in a normal way. Understand that children are going to fight, they are going to fuss, they are going to rebel, and they are going to have moments of anger. Do not try to make your child an adult. He is not a miniature adult. He is not a toy for you to show off; he is a child, an individual child. He is not like any other child that has ever been born. He is an individual. Try to understand him as an individual and accept him as an individual.

Try to direct a child's energy, thoughts, and his life. I like to think of a child as a very delicate musical instrument that must be played by the music that was written for that particular instrument. Because your child is unique, he is a very delicate musical instrument and there is no other musical instrument in the entire world like your child.

Don't play your music on the instrument that is your child. You play the music that was written for your child. This makes things difficult sometimes, because as a parent you must constantly search for the music that goes with your child.

Remember that your child is not a product of just you, but of your parents and your grandparents. Your child is a product of everyone he meets and every situation he is in. Every encounter makes a permanent change in his life, so accept your child as an individual.

I hear parents that are so proud of their little child because he "looks like a little adult." He always dresses just right, he always says the right things, and he always acts like a little adult. If this is what you think, then visit the mental hospital and you will find that many of the

9

people there are there because, as children, they were never allowed to be a child. They were always on display, always being showed off. Their parents pushed them too far until one day they went over the edge, and they could not be that little lady or little gentleman all the time!

Recognize that your child is not always going to say the right thing or do the right thing. Your child is an individual, a very precious individual, and a gift from God. Accept the individual traits and personalities of your child and do not try to raise your child to please anybody else. Raise your child according to his own abilities. Do not raise your child to feed your own ego or try to make your child into something that *you* would want them to be. Let your child find his own way in life. Let your child find what his temperament is geared for and explore his abilities, and not what brings prestige to you.

LOVE YOUR CHILD

Secondly, love your child. Love your child! There is nothing that can take the place of love. A lot of misguided parents today have the idea that they can show their love by buying expensive toys. You cannot show love by buying toys. Nothing takes the place of warmth, understanding and good old fashioned love.

When you feed your baby, hold your baby. Don't put him in the other room, prop up the bottle and shut the door. Hold your child close to you and give that child a sense of security, a sense of love. A lot of children grow up to be adults have failed to adjust in life. They are trying to find acceptance and love all their lives. They feel they were rejected as a child, and thus as adults, they still have a sense of insecurity. They are still fighting inner battles trying to find acceptance and love simply because nobody really cared when they were young.

Between 1900 and 1920, America had the highest infant mortality rate in the world. They began to study why so many babies died in America, especially in institutions and foster homes. In one foster home they found that every child under two years of age had died but one. They tried to find out why.

As part of the study, they went to Germany and visited some of the foster homes that had a low infant mortality rate. In these foster homes children had a person they called, "Mami." This was a lady that took care of the babies and children because the children didn't have a mother or dad. They had an elderly woman, who loved the babies and little children. She fed the babies, cared for the babies, and those children lived. In contrast, in America the foster children were dying.

Nothing will take the place of love, holding your child, coddling your child, and loving your child. Toys and expensive things will not take the place of love. We talk about deprived children and children living in poverty, and we find that some of the greatest poverty situations in America are not in terms of a lack of clothes and food, but in terms of a lack of love.

We think of underprivileged children as those who don't have nice clothes to wear. Maybe they go barefooted, they don't have enough to eat, their teeth are not cared for, or they don't receive medical attention. These are the deprived underprivileged people. I have come to realize that some of the most underprivileged children in America have a dozen pair of shoes, all the food they can eat, all the finest clothes to wear, and all that money can buy, but they are hungry and starving for love, just a little love.

You don't have to smother your child to love your child, but you can never give your child all the love he demands. You need to understand that children are little dictators. The more you things you give, the more they want. You have got to know how to give your child real love and understanding.

DISCIPLINE YOUR CHILD

When it comes to handling children, a third thing to remember is to discipline your child. Your child must be disciplined. Nothing can take the place of discipline. You say, "Well, I love my child too much to spank my child." But, if you love your child, you will spank your child when he needs it. You must show discipline and punishment if your child needs it. You must show the child correction and give that correction.

Suppose you got up in the morning and you discovered that all the stop signs in town had been removed. You ask, "Why did they remove all the stop signs?

Someone replies, "Well, the City Council met and they decided that they love the people of Gallatin, Tennessee so much that they removed all the stop signs and stop lights."

The novelty of it would be great for a little while, but it wouldn't be long before we would be crying for the stop signs and lights to be put back up. We know we need rules, we need restrictions, and we need guidance. It is not about love if our restrictions and rules are taken away. Real love puts on restrictions. Real love knows when to say, "No." Real love brings discipline.

A young teenage girl called me some time ago. She was in tears and crying because her folks were so mean to her. They were just awful! She wanted to go with some friends to Florida for Spring Break, and her parents said, "No." The girl just couldn't understand why. She was 16 years old, and certainly as a 16 year old she knew how to act in Florida. She just wanted to go.

The girl had left home and found a pay phone to call me. I talked to her awhile and I tried to find out why her parents were saying no. I asked, "Isn't it because they really love you and they want what's best for you? Now sure, they will make some mistakes, they won't always do the right thing, but basically, your parents' intent is always right. Out of love and care, they are saying, 'No.' Go home and put your arm around your mother and dad and say, 'Thank you for loving me enough to care what I do. Thank you enough for loving me enough to care where I stay, what I do, and who I go out with. Thank you for putting some rules down.'"

You see, children are really crying out for some rules. They need to be channeled and directed. There are two reasons for discipline. First of all, it tells your child he has worth in your eyes. It tells your children that you really care about them. Since you care, you make some rules, and you enforce those rules. You are firm in those rules. You have a right to know where your child is, who your child is with, and what your child is doing... because you care. The child needs this reassurance time and time again. Your child needs to know that mom and dad really care about them, and that's the reason why you sometimes say, "No."

The second reason for discipline is because when a child does wrong, he knows he does wrong. If you don't punish him, then guilt builds up inside that child and problems can develop later on. The punishment relieves the guilt. They will think, "I did something wrong, and I received punishment." Thus you can remove that guilt, and the child is happier and better adjusted because the guilt is taken care of.

There must some type of discipline. I realize that not every child needs to be spanked, but I haven't met one yet that didn't need it every now and then. "Experts" say that all children need is just a little pat on the back. I say, "Well yes! That's all they need if it's low enough and hard enough!" That kind of pat on the back will do the job because children have got to be taught that there are rules in life. Discipline is necessary. The Bible says,

> ***Proverbs 13:24*** He that spareth his rod hateth his son: but he that loveth him chasteneth him betimes.

> ***Proverbs 22:15*** Foolishness *is* bound in the heart of a child; *but* the rod of correction shall drive it far from him.

> ***Proverbs 23:13b*** ...Thou shalt beat him with the rod, and shalt deliver his soul from hell.

> ***Proverbs 29:15*** The rod and reproof give wisdom: but a child left *to himself* bringeth his mother to shame.

> ***Proverbs 29:17*** Correct thy son, and he shall give thee rest; yea, he shall give delight unto thy soul. Correct thy son, and he shall give thee rest; yea, he shall give delight unto thy soul.

Those are words of wisdom, taken from the Bible. Discipline is necessary and a child needs it, he cries out for it. Children are never too old for it, but you have to start young.

I don't know if this is true or not, but they say that the character and personality of a child is 50% developed by the time he is three years of age. You think about that. By the time he is five years of age, he is already 75% developed into the kind of person he is going to be. His character, his personality is developed. If he is rebellious at age five, then he will be rebellious as a teenager. If he talks back at age five, then he will talk back as a teenager. By age five, 75% of his character is already formed.

A lady came to a child psychiatrist or psychologist and asked, "When should I begin to teach my child about God?"

The fellow said, "How old is your child?"

And she said, "Well he is five years of age."

He exclaimed, "Lady, hurry home, you are already five years late!"

Don't let your children have everything they want. Don't pamper them; love them. Real love knows when to say, "No." Real love knows when to say, "Yes." Discipline your child.

My children may turn out to be the meanest people. They may already be the meanest children in town, but that doesn't change the Bible's precepts. That doesn't change the Word of God. Accept your child as an individual. They are very unique in the sight of God. Love your child with all your love, and remember, love is giving of yourself, not things. If you love your child, you will give yourself to your child. And again, discipline your child. Give direction and guidance to your child.

Children are pretty smart today. They can get ahead of you if you are not careful. You have to stay on your toes all the time and really love them.

I have a book that's been somewhat helpful to me. It's a thick book. The title is How to Father.[1] It looks at children in every stage of development. It talks about their characteristics.

The other night my oldest son came and in and said, "Daddy what does this word mean?" I passed it off and tried not to answer.

He came up with another question, "Daddy, what does this word mean?"

I asked, "Son, where did you get those words?"

He said, "Daddy, I have been reading your book, How to Father!"

Apparently he had been reading the book so he would know what he is supposed to be like as a son. I had been reading the book to know what I am supposed to be like as a dad. For the last two years, he had been ahead of me. I discovered that he had found my book and he had been reading it. We are getting along just fine, but what are we going to do now?

The best book to read is the Bible; the living Word. Use Christian precepts with your children. One of them is that you can't give your child too much love. You can't spoil your child with real love, so love your child, discipline your child, raise your child, and nurture your child in the things of God.

As I said earlier, there are no pat formulas. No two children are alike. I have two boys that are as different as day from night, and what will work with one, will not work with the other. If that's true in my home, in my situation, with two boys with two distinct personalities, then those two children must be dealt with in entirely different ways. I must accept them as being different. Other parents tell me the same

---

[1] How to Father, Fitzhugh Dodson, Signet; 1st edition (February 4, 1975), ISBN: 978-0451063083

thing too! Those who have large families agree that every child is different.

While there are no pat formulas for child rearing, nothing can take the place of acceptance, love, and discipline. Of course it goes without saying: set the right example for your child. Children learn more from those in their environment than from what we teach them in words only. They must "catch" the right way of doing things. They don't do that just from being told what the right thing is. I think children learn or "catch" religion in the home. Even if you don't teach it to them directly, they can "catch" it by the way you live.

Let me say to all of you, it is never too late to start. It is never too late to change. It's never too late for some of you to drop out of some of your social activities and other commitments, in order to spend more time with your children and more time with your family. It's never too late as long as your children are home. As long as they eat your food and put their feet under your table, you are their authority. God placed you in that position. You didn't; God did.

God says that you are the authority in the home. Fulfill that role as long as your children are with you. Biblically speaking, until your child marries, even if your child is 41 years old, the source of authority under God is the parent. When a child rebels against a parent, then the child rebels against God. It is just that simple. God has given you your position and role, and it is a tremendous responsibility. Children need to understand that you parents have been given a role from God. You have been given authority.

Children, listen to your parents, obey them, and if they are wrong, God will take care of them. You don't have to worry about it. Give God time to change their minds before you rebel. Parents may make hasty decisions from time to time. They are human and they make mistakes. When they make a mistake, don't go off half-cocked. Give God time to change their minds, and you will never regret it.

Dr. Harold W. Allen

CHAPTER 2: PATTERNS FOR PARENTS

First Baptist Church, Gallatin, Tennessee
<u>May 8, 1977</u>

Parenthood is an awesome responsibility. I think this is the reason that God gave such clear instructions on how to raise children.

> ***Proverbs 22:6*** Train up a child in the way he should go: and when he is old, he will not depart from it.

I like the emphasis on "the way he should go," rather than the way *they* should go. It recognizes the individuality of each child, and thus it recognizes each child is precious and individual. You must train each child differently, but you must have some basic fundamental principles that guide you.

Now, I realize that there are a lot of people telling you how to raise children today. And you wonder, "Could this be right?" I know what the psychologists say, and I know how they feel about spanking, about discipline, and about letting the little one express himself. But, let's look to the Word of God and see what God has to say about raising a child. I think the Bible's principles are timeless. They are ageless. God, knowing our nature and knowing the nature of your children, laid down some principles that will help you as parents for raising your child.

A TEACHING RESPONSIBILITY

I think, first of all, your responsibility as a parent is to teach your child. Training implies a teaching responsibility. You are to teach your child many different things. You are to teach your child about God, about his fellow man, about authority, how to be unselfish, about love, how to be honest, and how to be truthful. These are great responsibilities. They are teaching responsibilities.

17

We delegate so many things today, and we have come to be the generation of delegating everything. We delegate our child to the school, so that they might teach him. We send him to the library, so that he might get his books. We send him to the park, so that he might have his recreation. We send him to the movies for his entertainment. And, we send him to church for his religious training. Yet God says that the place teaching begins is in the home. You cannot delegate your responsibility for training and teaching your child about life to other people. You cannot delegate some of the basic principles that need to be applied as you teach your child.

Your child is going to ask you a thousand and one questions before he gets to be a teenager. And then, he is going to ask you more questions. You have opportunities to teach that a teacher does not have. You have opportunities to teach that the church does not have.

Did you know that your child is going to have 108,000 waking hours before he is grown? 108,000 waking hours! If he goes to school every day, he'll spend 7,000 of those hours in school. If he goes to church every time the doors are open, he'll spend around 1,000 hours in the church. That means he has 100,000 hours when he is awake. Those are your hours; hours when your child is your responsibility to teach. 100,000 hours for you to use or to neglect.

Let's not blame the church when the child turns out bad. Let's not blame the school when the child turns out bad. The school only has him for 7,000 hours, the church has him for 1,000 hours, and the home is responsible for that child for 100,000 hours. Those hours make up the years of development when your child can learn about life, and when he can learn to be honest, truthful, and faithful. When he is learning to be kind, considerate and understanding, he's at home.

What a responsibility you have! When he asks you questions, take time to answer them. Don't shove him off to somebody else. Stop what you are doing, read to your child, talk to your child, play with your child, and go places with your child. Answer their questions as they grow and get a little older, because they have so many questions. You teach them by right principles, but you also teach them, more importantly, by example. For a long time, they are going to listen to what you say, but when they see that your life is not consistent with what you say, they are going to shut you out. They want to see these things that you would teach them lived before them and lived in the home.

Couple of years ago a friend gave me a pipe for Christmas. I never smoked in my life, but I had been gaining a little weight since I passed the age of 40. I had been eating a little too much, and I snacked a lot a night. I thought, "Well, maybe if I smoked I wouldn't snack so much and wouldn't gain so much weight."

So I had this new pipe and a sack of tobacco that my friend gave me. I filled up my pipe and got it lit. I got a book and settled down to start smoking the pipe. My boy came in and he walked by, and then he turned around and did a double-take.

My boy said, "Daddy, what are you doing?"

I said, "Well, son, I am smoking."

He said, "Ohhhh, you are not!"

I said, "Yeah, I'm going to smoke!"

He responded, "Daddy, NO! You can't smoke!"

I said, "Well yeah, son, it's alright. I'm just gonna smoke at home and just while I am reading and studying, so I won't snack… and it'll be good for me. I think it will kind of take care of some of my nervous energy."

My son exclaimed, "No Daddy! No, you are not going to smoke!"

I said, "Yeah, son, I think I am going to take up smoking."

Well, I was really serious, and he left. He came back a little later and he said, "Daddy, I guess it's alright for me to smoke, isn't it?"

I said, "What do you mean?"

He said, "Well, Daddy if you can smoke, then I can smoke."

I took the pipe and put it away and it hasn't been out since. I could have told him that I'm older, I'm more mature, and that older people do things that children cannot do. I could have told him that because I am older, I can drink. I could have told him that because I'm older, I can smoke. I could have told him that because I'm older I can use profanity, but he can't do it!

No, you can't fool kids anymore. They know there are some basic principles. And, if smoking is harmful to their health, it's also harmful to your health. If drinking is wrong for them, then it's wrong for you. If using God's name in vein is wrong for them, it's wrong for you. They know this, and they understand this.

A father was outside one day. A tornado came by and he said to the neighbor, "There's goes a blankety blank tornado." And his little four year old son ran in the house and said, "Mommy, mommy, there goes a blankety blank tornado!" The son didn't know what the words meant, but he had a good teacher. He learned at the age of four how to curse, at home.

I realize children are going to learn some things away from home. They are going to learn to smoke some, maybe to drink some, maybe to curse some. But, you are going to have them more than the world is going to have them in those early formative years. Make sure that you offer something to counteract and counter-balance what they hear everywhere else. Do it by example, with an example of love, of concern, and of understanding.

A father came downstairs one Sunday morning. He was dressed to go to the golf course, as he did every Sunday morning. His adolescent son was home and the father was shocked. He turned to his son and said, "Son, why didn't you go to Sunday school?"

The boy said, "Daddy, I'm not going to Sunday school anymore."

The dad replied, "What do you mean you are not going to Sunday school anymore?"

The boy explained, "Well, daddy, you don't go to Sunday school. Evidently, it's not good for you, so I am not going to go anymore! I am going to stay home today."

The father didn't say anything. He went upstairs. He took off his golf outfit and put on his suit. The father came down and said, "Son, let's go to Sunday school."

Hand in hand they went to church, and the boy was happy because he was going to Sunday school with his father. Years later when that boy was ordained as a minister, someone remarked, "I wonder where you would be today if your father had gone on to the golf course that Sunday."

Example, influence; these are what you have! Children know what is important by what you emphasize in your life. What is important to you? Is church important to you? If so, it will be important to your child, but if it isn't, then your child will learn that by your example.

You have responsibility. In those 100,000 hours your child is at home, you are going to have your child in your care to teach, and you can teach them by what you say. That is important, but you are also going to teach them by what you do and who you are.

A DISCIPLINING RESPONSIBILITY

The Bible says to discipline your child. Now, I realize there are a lot of questions about spanking a child. Psychologists say that spanking is child beating. Scolding is brow beating. Discipline is just a parental tantrum, which gets rid of the frustration of the parent. Well, that's what they say, but don't you believe it for a minute. Your child has a little bit of devil in him or her, I can assure you. It's there, and you've got to discipline that child to train that child.

Some people or psychologists say that whipping a child doesn't change the child. The child still has the same inner drive, the same inner needs, and the same attitudes, and that might be true. Maybe the outward physical spanking is not going to change the inner child. It will, however, do this: it will create an atmosphere in which you can teach the child and the change the inner person.

There is an old story about a man that sold a horse. All you had to do was say, "Giddy up!", and the horse would go. A neighbor tried to get the horse to go and it wouldn't go. He went to his friend and complained because the horse wouldn't move when he said, "Giddy up!" The horse just stood there.

The man replied, "It'll go!" He picked up a 2 x 4 and hit the horse in the head and the horse took off.

The friend said, "I thought all you have to say is, 'Giddy up,' and it'd go!"

The man said, "That's right, but first you have to teach it."

Sometimes in child discipline, you have to get their attention. I don't mean to child-beat them. I don't mean to hit them over the head with a 2 x 4, but I do mean that you must get their attention through discipline, and then they listen. Then, you can teach them.

God has an awful lot to say about discipline. God is a heavenly Father, and He gives the example for us. God disciplines us, God chastises us, and God spanks His children, in order that He might get our attention. He doesn't change us. You see, sometimes He puts us flat on our backs, just so we'll listen. Sometimes crisis comes into our lives so that He can create an atmosphere in which we will listen.

God sees raising a family the same way. Discipline creates an atmosphere in which a child can be taught. Just to spank your child and walk off does more harm than good. You have created the atmosphere, but have done nothing with it. So, God will say, "Create the atmosphere, and then when the child is all eyes and ears and waiting, give him some love. Give him some understanding. Give him some firmness, and give him some explanation on why you did what you did. Because you love your children, because you are fearful for their safety, and because you want them to turn out good, spank them to get their attention. And then, after every spanking, give them love, a lot of love and teach them the lesson you are trying to teach them. Discipline doesn't hurt."

A grandmother went to visit her grandchildren and when she came back somebody asked, "Well, did you spoil your grandchildren?"

She said, "You know you can't spoil a baby with love." You spoil a baby by not disciplining a baby or a child. You can't spoil children with love. Give them an abundance of love. Children get spoiled because they are not disciplined. They aren't spoiled because they have too much love. Give them love, a lot of love. You grandparents give them love too, but grandparents, give them some discipline too, if you have to... provided it's alright with your daughter-in-law or son-in-law. Still, do love and restrain your grandchildren.

The Bible says,

> ***1 Samuel 3:13*** For I have told him that I will judge his house for ever for the iniquity which he knoweth; because his sons made themselves vile, and he restrained them not.

God said that he would curse the house of Eli because his sons made themselves vile, and Eli did not restrain them. His sons made themselves vile and Eli, the priest, did not restrain them. Eli the priest did not exercise discipline over his own sons!

> ***Proverbs 13:24*** He that spareth his rod hateth his son: but he that loveth him chasteneth him betimes.

He who spareth the rod, he who fails to give discipline really hates his son or his daughter. If you love your children, you will train them, you will teach them, and you will discipline them.

> ***Proverbs 19:18*** Chasten thy son while there is hope, and let not thy soul spare for his crying.

Don't get uptight or feel guilty because your children cry when you discipline them. Don't feel guilty about being the "boss." I think your child needs to know that someone is in the house is stronger, older, more mature, and is wiser than is he or she. That's your responsibility. There is nothing wrong with asserting yourself. You don't have to beg, plead or apologize to your children to try to get them to do things. Assert yourself as a parent and do not worry much about their crying. They are usually not hurting that much. I used to cry more before a spanking than when I got a spanking. I was thinking that maybe I might cry myself out of a spanking!

> ***Proverbs 22:15*** Foolishness *is* bound in the heart of a child; *but* the rod of correction shall drive it far from him.

Foolishness is bound in the heart of a child. The rod of correction should drive it far from him. Foolishness is there. Everybody has to climb up the "fool's hill." That is what the Bible says. The only way you can drive the foolishness out of his heart is through discipline.

> ***Proverbs 23:13a*** Withhold not correction from the child: for *if* thou beatest him with the rod, he shall not die....

Your child will act like he is going to die, but he is not going to die.

> ***Proverbs 23:13b*** ...Thou shalt beat him with the rod, and shalt deliver his soul from hell.

The Bible has a lot to say about the rod. Psychologists do say this, and maybe there is something to it: do not use your hand to spank because your hand is not detached from you.

When you keep smacking with your hand, your children see you doing it. When you pick up the flyswatter, the belt, the yard stick, or whatever and give it two or three passes, you lay that down. You pick it up; you lay it down. Detach yourself from it. Thus, your children see the rod as an instrument of correction, and not your hand. I don't know as that is what psychologists say to do. But, it really makes sense when you think about it: to detach the rod. God always talks about the rod and using the rod. God speaks of picking up the rod and laying down the rod. Just as the rod is apart from Him, it is also to be apart from you.

I know they say you need to let a child express himself, but there is foolishness in the child's heart. Psychologists say that if you have a can of red paint, a child will get in it and splatter it all over the room. They say that's alright! They say you should just love him and don't do anything about it because you might warp him and his little personality. Well, there is something that needs to be warped if a child does such things, and it's not his personality. My mother never read a book on psychology, and if I had done that with the paint, I know where I would have been warped!

Someone said, "My child is alright. All he needs is a pat on the back now and then."

The preacher said, "Well, that's alright, if it's low enough and hard enough!"

And that's what God says. A pat on the back is alright every now and then… if it's low enough and hard enough. As parents we've got to be restrained, we've got to be disciplined, and we've got to know what's right. We need to know what we can do and cannot do, and children need this. They are looking for it. If they don't learn to respect authority in the home, they are not going to respect authority anywhere else. If they don't learn to respect the authority of mommy and daddy, they are not going to respect the laws of the land. They are not going to respect their teachers. They are not going to respect others that they have to work with later in life, and their life is going to be miserable. They have got to learn at home.

When they do get a spanking at school, and by the way the Supreme Court says it's alright now for the teacher to spank your child, don't try to get the teacher fired.* Don't talk about your child's school teacher in front of your child.

When I was growing up, I would have been spanked when I came home, if I had received a spanking at school. I am not suggesting that you go that far, but realize and recognize that your child is not always perfect away from home. Sometimes he needs some correction away from home. I know you are smiling because if you know my boys, you know how they are away from home. Children need discipline sometimes. Discipline is good. There is nothing wrong with it. But, discipline your child in love, in firmness, and in fairness.

Do not make a mistake that I made on occasion, like many parents do. Sometimes I let my children go so far that they got on my nerves. I would get uptight and all of the sudden I would explode. And in the anger, I punished them, and that is wrong. Don't whip your child when you're angry with your child. Go in another room and get your anger settled down. Get calmed down, because discipline is not a means of punishing the child. It must be a means of teaching your child. You don't teach your child a thing when you explode and attack them like

---

* At the time of this sermon, spanking was legal in school. As of the time of this publication, spanking is no longer legal in school.

you are going to kill them. They don't learn anything in that experience.

A LOVING RESPONSIBILITY

Finally, love your child. This is the third basic principle from the Bible.

You must teach and train your child. It's all through the Scripture, from Genesis to Revelation. You have the responsibility. We got uptight a few years ago when the Supreme Court said you couldn't read the Bible in school. Well, they didn't really say that, but that's the way it's been interpreted by many school boards. They didn't say you couldn't pray in school, but that's the way many school boards interpreted a local lower court decision. Regardless, we got all uptight over that decision.

The point is that it never was the school's place to pray and teach your child religion and read the Bible. Nowhere does the Bible delegate this responsibility. It's always the home. We have no right to get uptight, because it is a parental responsibility: to teach your child and to raise your child in the nurturing admonition of the Lord. It's not the school's responsibility. So, teach your child to know God, to love God, and to receive Christ as Savior. Discipline your child, so that they might go in the right way. Train him up in the way that he should go and when he's old he won't part from it.

Of the 21 men that defected during the Korean Conflict, a survey was done concerning their home life. It was determined that the defectors were unloved at home!

Did you know that according to another survey, 67% of a toddler's waking hours are spent in front of a television set? 67% of a toddler's waking hours are spent with a mechanical parent; a mechanical babysitter.

Over 50% of all mothers in America, who have children under 18 years of age, work away from home. This means that over 50% of children come home to a mechanical babysitter, and then the mom and dad finally come home. They come home growling, grumpy, tired, disgusted, griping, and put a meal on the table. They dress the kid for bed, so they can have a few minutes to rest and relax.

If you can work, then fine. Some of you need to work and it's good. You need to work for financial reasons. Maybe you need to work for other reasons, such as for your own sense of well-being. Perhaps you must work because you don't want to lose your person and your individuality. Fine, but don't do it at the expense of loving your children. Children still need time to cuddle with you. They still need time to crawl up in your arms. They need love.

One of the greatest inventions, I guess, for the modern mother was the baby bottle. It is the worst thing for the child. The child needs the comfort and love of their mother. So, use the bottle on occasion. It is great because, with a bottle, daddy can also feed and rock the baby. Hold that baby, feed that baby, and love that baby with all the love you can spare; holding, squeezing, and cuddling that baby. Sometimes, even in the morning, when your toddler is walking, let them come in the bedroom with you and cuddle up for 30 minutes or so. Or, do it for 15 minutes before you get up, but love on your child.

This reminds me of a story I heard a long time ago, about a farmer and his wife living in the Ozarks. They had a very bright young boy. They sent him off to the State University. The time came for the boy to graduate, and they had never been to the State University. They got dressed up. The father put on his suit, and it was shiny with wear. The mother got her best dress out. They made the trip to the State University. They sat in the back of the auditorium and waited. The graduation exercises started and their son was recognized. He was the valedictorian of the class. He was a brilliant young man. He gave a speech that night, and he spoke with smoothness and eloquence. They sat there in the back and listened to their son as he spoke. Finally, the father, with tears rolling down his cheeks, turned to his wife and he said, "Ma, I believe that is the best crop we ever grew. That's the best crop we ever grew."

May it be said of you parents in years to come, that your son, your daughter, is the best crop you ever grew.

Our Father God, we are grateful for this time of sharing together. We are thankful for parents. We are thankful for grandparents, who are here. We thank You for the children that have been dedicated to You. May they continue to grow in wisdom, in stature, and in favor with You in mind. Amen.

Dr. Harold and Nancy Allen. Dr. Allen is holding their son, Stephen. Nancy is holding their son, David.

Chapter 2: Patterns for Parents

CHAPTER 3: HONOR FATHER AND MOTHER

First Baptist Church, Gallatin, Tennessee
February 10, 1980

If anything, it may be old fashion, outdated, or archaic that children must honor their father and mother. But, this concept is just as relevant today as it was when the Eternal God first spoke about it. It is to be applied to our lives.

God has given us tools for living. God says that if we abide by these rules, then we will have a happy, successful and fulfilled life. Disregard these rules, cast them aside, and you will suffer the consequences.

The first four Commandments (Deuteronomy 5:7-11) have to do with reverence for God. God is holy and worthy of our worship, our reverence, and our service. The last six Commandments (Deuteronomy 5:12-21) deal with respect for our fellow man.

How we can live together in a society without it being one of chaos and confusion which would destroy itself? God tells us that respect for our fellow man starts with the basic fundamental basic unit of society: the home... the family.

MOTHER AND FATHER – THE BASIC UNIT OF SOCIETY

> ***Deuteronomy 5:16*** Honour thy father and thy mother, as the LORD thy God hath commanded thee; that thy days may be prolonged, and that it may go well with thee, in the land which the LORD thy God giveth thee.

Honor and give weight, consideration, reverence, and respect to your parents. Long before God established the church, long before He established the schools, long before government was introduced, God established the home: the basic unit of society.

God has given us some rules that go back to that fundamental unit of society, the very foundational rock of society. God says that in the family structure, there are to be parents, as well as children who honor and respect their parents. This is the very foundation of any society.

The children of Israel could not earn their way to the promise land. They had to build their nation. God told them that if their nation was to provide for them, then they must come back to the basic principles of honor and respect of those in authority over the people.

God did not speak of a promise to an individual. He didn't mean that if they showed honor and respect to their father that they would live to be old. God was speaking to the nation, Israel. God was saying that if the nation was to survive, the nation must understand, respect, and honor roles within the home. That is where respect is to be taught. That is where authority is to be learned. It applied to Israel, and it applies to us too.

The home is where we develop personalities and learn how to live together. The Jews sought to live by this. Though 4,000 years have passed, Israel is still a nation! 2,000 of those years they lived without a land and without a country. They were cast out in all parts of the world, but they held to the fundamental unit of the home as being the family. They taught respect for authority for the family, honor for the family, and for the most part they married within their culture. They practiced their religion.

Today they are back in their land with their own independent flag flying over Israel. No nation in history has been able to survive when it was disbursed into other nations. Other peoples intermarried, and they lost their national identity. They ceased to be a nation, but not the Jews. This happened for the Jews because they came back to this basic fundamental promise... if they would honor their parents, respect the wishes of their parents, obey their parents, and learn from their parents, they would survive as a nation. And, God would bless them.

I think God is saying that same message to America. He is saying that if America is to survive, we've got to come back to the home. The home must be the foundation rock of our society, where we instill the moral fiber for our society. We have to reestablish authority and respect in the home. It's not the schools' responsibility to teach authority, respect and good manners, or religion! It's the home's place. It's not the church's responsibility to take the religious instruction of the children as its primary responsibility. It's the home's responsibility. This is where authority is learned.

Rome fell. Rome fell not because of invading armies, not because of forces outside, but because the home failed. Rome ceased to be a great power. Our greatest fear today should not be communist Russia.[*] We may get uptight about it, and we may talk about the draft and increasing our military might. We might send our Navy and our Army across the waters to protect us, and rightfully, those things are of vital interest to America. But, our greatest threat is not communist Russia. Our greatest threat is the breakup of the home, where there should be authority, love, and respect. Where the home goes, there too goes the nation. God laid down a very fundamental law. If America, or any nation, is to survive, it must learn respect in the home. The family unit must stay together! The family must be a family against all outside things that would destroy the home.

WHY CHILDREN MUST HONOR PARENTS

Children, honor your parents! Honor them because they know more than you know. I know that is difficult to conceive in our day, when the child is exposed to so much in school, on the TV, on the radio, through the news and when parents work a lot as the child grows up. The child may know much more from a school book, but they haven't lived many experiences.

Sometimes the "school of hard knocks" is a better school than the school of higher education. Children, your parents have been "the pack ahead of you." They know some of the dangers, some of the pitfalls, and some of the problems. They know more because they have lived longer than you, and that stands to reason.

I said to my 17 year old son the other day, "Son, do you know more than your younger brother?"

And he replied, "Sure I do."

And I said, "Why?"

And he said, "Because I am older."

And then I had him; I knew I had him. I said, "Then son, by that reasoning, I know much more than you because I am much older than you," and his expression changed.

---

[*] This sermon was given during the time of the Cold War, when America and Russia were competing superpowers, seeing one another as threats in the world.

My son wasn't willing to give full acceptance to that truth, but he knew I had knowledge through my years. He knew I had learned some things by trial and error that he had not learned, because I had lived longer. I had experienced more, and thus had the right to tell him some things because of my experience.

I have always liked a statement by Mark Twain. He said that when he was 16 he thought his father was the most ignorant man that ever lived. When Mr. Twain turned 21, he was amazed how much his father had learned in 5 years!

It's a shame that we don't recognize a little earlier that our parents know more than we know. At the age of 10, most children think their parents know everything. By the time they are 16, they know their parents don't know anything, and they know everything. By the time they are 19, they are beginning to waiver a little bit, and they start to think maybe their parents weren't all wrong. By the time they are 25 and 26, they begin to realize that their parents were perfect and knew everything, and they begin to praise their parents for all the knowledge their parents had for those critical years between ages 16 and 21, which were difficult. Teenagers are not willing to acknowledge that their parents know more, but they do. They know more because they lived longer.

It stands to reason that a 30 year old woman knows more than a 10 year old girl. It stands to reason that a 40 year old man knows more than a 15 year old boy, just because the man has lived longer.

So, children are to honor their parents because the parents know more. Children are to honor them because God said to honor them. God has placed parents as the source of authority in the home. They are God's representatives in the home.

God established the home back in the Garden of Eden. And, in each family unit he put a head to that family unit. He delegated authority to those parents, and they are God's representatives in the home. That's God's authority in the home. When you disobey your parents, when you show disrespect to your parents, or when you dishonor your parents, you are disobeying the Lord. You are showing disrespect to God, dishonor to God, and disobedience to God! So if you want to be a Christian person, a Christian young person, you will honor your parents because God placed them in authority over you. If you don't learn their authority, if you don't learn respect for them, then your lives will be a miserable failure. You will have problems adjusting throughout your life. God has placed the parents there to teach children some things and to be the child's source of authority.

How Children Can Honor Parents

So, how do you honor your parents? When you are young and are growing up, you honor them by obeying them. Parents may not always be right. In fact, many times they may be wrong. Your parents may, at times, be old fashioned, old fogies, and they may not be up with the times, but they are your parents. Even though they may make wrong decisions, they do what they do out of love, out of concern and care for you. And thus, when they tell you something, you obey them.

If your parents ask you to be home by 10 pm, then you be home by 10 pm, or you call and let them know why cannot make it home. If you tell them you are going to someone's house, you go there. If you change your mind, and decide to go somewhere else, then you call and let them know that you want to change your plans, and you get permission to go. Do this as long as you stay at home.

I know sometimes teenagers think they have the right to do their own thing, but they only have the right to do their own thing as the parents give them that right. That freedom is one God has entrusted to the parents to grant. The purpose is so that the parents can build "a hedge or fence" around the children, to restrain them, to discipline them, and to teach them. Children must learn authority, respect, and honor.

Children, do not cause your parents unnecessary worry by disobeying them, by doing things that you know are contrary to their will and wish for you. Your parents have laid down some fundamental, basic principles for you to live by, and you know it. To openly violate that, or to disregard that, is dishonoring them and the Lord. So, obey your parents.

Your parents feed you. They clothe you, they send you to school, they care for you, they give you spending money, and in return you honor them by obeying their wishes and their desires for you, even though at times it may hurt. If it hurts you, you can be sure it's hurting your parents that much more. Sometimes your parents make a decision because they know it is right for you. They see you hurt, and they hurt inside too. Sometimes we parents give in because we don't like to see you hurt so much, even though we know giving in is not good for you. Still, we sometimes do it because we can't stand to hurt when you hurt; we love you. Thus, parents make rules and regulations for your benefit and out of concern for you. So, children, obey your parents.

A way to honor your parents is to obey them when you are growing up, and then support them when you are older. As you get older and have your own family, then of course, your parents are older. They may need some support, some care, some encouragement, and some concern. So, you support them.

As your parents get older, maybe irritable or a little overbearing at times, continue to support them. There may come a time when you have to put them in a nursing home because that may be the best thing for them and for the family. That is good and well, if you are doing it with the right motivation. It is good if you are doing it because you care for them and love them and you want the very best for them, but if you are doing it just to get them out of your hair, out of your home and away from you so you can have your own freedom, then it would be wrong. If you are doing it for your own convenience, then it would be wrong. Be sure you check your motivation if you send them off to live in a nursing home.

Many times, in modern days, sending older parents off to a nursing home may be the logical and the practical thing to do, but at the same time, their welfare should be upper most in your mind at all times. As you get older and have that charge and responsibility, you may have to carry them from room to room. Remember, there was a time when they carried you from room to room. You may have to feed them with a spoon when they get old, but remember there was a time when they fed you, and you spit up on them. There was a time when you didn't swallow the food. You put it in your mouth and spit it out, and they kept feeding you because they knew that you needed the food. You may have to bathe your parents, clothe them, and put them to bed, but remember there was a time when they clothed you, they bathed you, they changed your diaper, and they put you to bed. They rocked you and stayed up all night with you, holding your hand, taking you to the doctor and caring for you. This is the way you pay for your raising really. You honor your parents in their old age. You see that their needs are met, and you give them support and encouragement. That is what families are for.

This past weekend, in Wisconsin, I saw a family support one another in a time of sorrow, a time of crisis, and a time of death.** How wonderful it was to see those who made an effort to be there when their father was sick. He was critical for 16 weeks, yet time and time

---

** This refers to a death in the family of Dr. Allen's wife's aunt. Etta Brandl was Nancy Allen's aunt. Etta's husband, Martin Brandl, had died. His boys (Jim and Bill – who were Nancy's cousins) were very supportive during that time. Their example meant a lot to Dr. Allen.

again they made the long journey to be there by his side. How wonderful it was to see those who held their father's hand, cared for him, fed him, and did what they could do. When he died, they could go to the funeral without any regrets, and they could stand there knowing they did what they could. Those two boys stood there to give support to their mother, to encourage her and to see that her needs were met during that time of sorrow in the home. I thought, "That is what a family is for. That is the way it ought to be. You stand together, you stick together, and you support one another in hours of grieving."

Children don't be so ungrateful that you don't have time for your parents when they become old. Show them love, consideration, support and, all times, you respect your parents. Whether young or old, you respect them; you honor them.

Ham's sin was that he laughed at his father, Noah (Genesis 9:21-26). You see, Noah got drunk, which was wrong. Noah was naked in his tent, which was wrong. Noah made a ridiculous sight for his children, and that was wrong. I cannot uphold Noah and what he did. He was wrong, but Ham looked upon him, laughed and made fun of his father in his drunken stupor. And, God came to curse Ham.

Ham's descendants became servants to other peoples because of what he had done. He showed disrespect to his father. Noah was his father and he was to respect him, regardless of what his father did or how he lived. Ham became the forerunner of a people that became a servant people. They are a servant people even to this day. To this day they are still a servant people and always will be serving people, because of Ham's lack of respect for his father. God takes this "honor your father and mother" commandment seriously, and we are to take it seriously. We are to honor our parents and respect them at all times.

A WORD TO PARENTS ABOUT BEING HONORED BY CHILDREN

I think there is a word here for parents, too. I think God is saying to the parents, "Be worthy of that honor. Be worthy of that respect."

Parents, live right before your children; know Christ as your own Savior. Lead your son and daughter to know Christ as his or her Savior. Be a worthy example. Be considerate of your children. Recognize them as individuals, and try to love each one as an individual. Do not expect more of a child than the child can produce. At all times, be the model for your child to follow after. Be the model, so they will walk in your footsteps.

Parents, discipline your children in love, do not punish. I think sometimes we get it all turned around, and so we want to beat our children when they do wrong. God wouldn't say to beat your child or punish your child. God has a lot to say about discipline in love.

The word *discipline* means to teach a lesson. We need to discipline our children, in order that they might learn some valuable lessons, some moral lessons, and to be what God would have them to be. God is saying to parents, to all of us, to be the right kind of parent, who would be worthy of honor and respect. We must do this by living the right kind of life, and by inviting Christ into our hearts and lives, and by loving our children.

There is much more to be said on this commandment to honor the father and mother; it is about the home and the family. There are many more sermons that could be preached about the home and the family. I think we have lost track of what God intended for the home to be, and of the love that should be in a home, and in family ties. We are going in so many separate ways today. Everyone has their own interests, their own thing, and we are breaking up the home.

The word *broken* was never meant to apply to the home. The home was never to be fragmented or broken up. The home was to be together, a family unit, praying together and playing together, and doing things together. We often have our own thing. I think sometimes we get involved in good things, but they become wrong because they take us away from the family. I think a family ought to have some type of unity. I think you ought to laugh together, you ought to cry together, you ought to worship together, and you ought to stay together.

Parents, spend some time with your children. Many parents are too busy, doing too many clubs, doing too many committee meetings, getting too caught up in sports, too caught up this business or that business. So, our children have to grow up the best way they can, sometimes without the love and care of parents. Some of us need to resign some things, redesign our schedules, and give some time to the family, to the children.

You don't have very long in life, and if you don't do things with children when they are 9, 10, 11 years of age, don't expect them to do anything with you when they are 15, 16, 17 years of age. They won't have time for you. You have to have time for them when they are growing up, or when they get older they won't have any time for you. They'll have their own thing. It's important to spend time with your children, love your children, to support your children, to stand with your children and you lead your children to know Christ.

Dr. Harold and Nancy Allen

Chapter 3: Honor Father and Mother

CHAPTER 4: GOD'S PATTERN FOR PARENTS

First Baptist Church, Gallatin, Tennessee
<u>May 14, 1989</u>

Being a parent is an awesome responsibility. It is a difficult and challenging career. It takes a lot of creativity, discipline, and imagination to be a good parent.

Before I had children I had several sermons on how to be good parents. I had a sermon titled, "10 Rules for Raising Good Kids." I could speak with great authority because I had my first child, David.

After David came, I changed that sermon. I compiled it with others and called it, "Helpful Hints for Raising Children." Then, Stephen came along and I changed the sermon to "Feeble Suggestions from a Fellow Struggling Parent."

Then during my boys' teen years, I forgot about preaching on being a parent. I threw my sermons on parenthood away. I discovered several things. First of all, there is not a set formula for raising children. There are no simple solutions. There is nothing dogmatically that we can say such as, "This is the way you raise a perfect child or a good child." Every child is unique and different. Every child has different concepts, different thinking, and requires a different approach. Every child has a different personality.

God doesn't create any two babies alike. He doesn't create any two people alike. Your baby is special, precious and unique. There never has been, and never will be, another baby just like your baby. So, what may work with one child may not work with another child. I discovered there is no way to raise a child without any problems, without some rebellion, without some pulling away, and without some struggling to grow up.

A child seeks to be independent, and to be his or her own person. As a result, a lot of the "cock-sureness" was knocked out of me when I was trying to raise my boys. I came to realize that even though there's no one formula for raising children, there are some common principles. There are some guidelines and patterns for raising children.

A GIFT WITH RESPONSIBILITY AND ROLES

I think, first of all, we must recognize that a child is a responsibility from God; a gift from God. You have a responsibility as a parent.

Society is going to make you fulfill some of those responsibilities. Society says that you must see that your child has healthcare, and the system will take you to court if you withhold healthcare from your child. Society says you must send your child to school to get an education… that is a must. Society says that you must feed your child, that you most clothe your child, and that you must shelter your child. If you are not willing to do these as a parent, then society will take your child from your home and place the child in a foster home.

I know that you are going to fulfill those responsibilities, even if you might have to go without on occasion. You may have to sacrifice to see that your child gets a good education, the best medical care, and the best dental care. You will see that your child gets good clothes, the designer clothes sometimes. Do without yourselves when necessary.

You want your child to be dressed as well as any other child in town, and you are going to do that, but there is a responsibility that we overlook sometimes. That is the responsibility we have to God, not just to society and our children, but to God.

I believe that children are a gift from God. I believe that God placed your children in your home for a special purpose, a special reason. I don't believe babies are ever an accident. Regardless of what some may say, I believe there is a divine God Who is controlling the life that comes into your home. He places that baby into your home for a reason and for a purpose.

When your child is born and you learn and accept the responsibility, then perhaps you might read that little book, Angel Unaware.[2] I think every person ought to read it. It was written back in the fifties. I've read it since then several times. It is a lovely, lovely story. It is a story written by Dale Evans Rogers.

The story is about a little angel that came to live in a family's home for a little while. The little angel came as a severely handicapped, Downs Syndrome child, who died and went back to heaven. The imagery is of a little baby reporting back to God after completing her mission on earth. It is a story of a baby girl named

---

[2] Angel Unaware, Dale Evans Rogers, Fleming H. Revell Co.; 1st edition (1953), Amazon ASIN: B0007DMEEA

Robin Elisabeth, and how she transformed the lives of the Roy Rogers family.

Their baby came in this world with an appalling handicap. I believe within all my heart that God sent her on a two-year mission to their home to strengthen us all spiritually and to draw us closer together in knowledge, love, and fellowship with God.

Mr. Rogers' wife said, "It has been said that the tragedy and sorrow never leave us when they find us. In this instance, both Roy and I are grateful to God for the privilege of learning some great lessons of truth though his tiny messenger, Robin Elisabeth Rogers. It is Robin's story. It is what her mother believed Robin told her Heavenly Father shorty after 8pm on August 24, 1952 - a precious, precious account of her journey on earth. Somehow I believe the story speaks to situations when a child is severely handicapped, and when a child is bright and healthy. They have been sent on a divine mission to your home to teach you some lessons. Yes, children are a gift from God. What is the responsibility of a parent?"[3]

Parents Have The Responsibility To Teach

The responsibility I think of first, as parents, is to teach.

> ***Deuteronomy 6:7*** And thou shalt teach them diligently unto thy children, and shalt talk of them when thou sittest in thine house, and when thou walkest by the way, and when thou liest down, and when thou risest up.

Teach your children. Teach them at night when they lie down. Tell them a bedtime story. Teach them in the morning when they get up - have a prayer of thanksgiving for the nights rest. Teach them as you walk along the path in Peachtree City. Point out the trees, birds and the grass. Tell them how God made these things. Teach them day in and day out. You have that responsibility. You cannot delegate it to anyone else. It is not the school's responsibility to teach your child right and wrong. I long for the day we have schools that teach morals and ethics, right and wrong. I wish we had more of those today, but even if we had the very best system, the church and the schools do not relieve you, or me, as parents from teaching our children right and wrong.

---

[3] ibid.

Children learn at home the great truths they learn. They have been learning before they start school. Many of the things that they're going to live by in life they will learn before they are five years of age. They learn attitudes, and they learn anger, fear, and frustration before they are five years of age. They learn a working vocabulary before they start school. These things will carry them all through life. Children learn at home, and the time you spend with them helps them learn some great principles.

You need to teach them God's Word. Tell and read Bible stories to them. Share with them, even while they are at the age when you still hold them in your arms. They will be still long enough. Read them a story at night. Read to them, talk to them, and share with them the great stories from years ago… like when we had the old <u>McGuffey's Readers</u> in school.[4]

Children did a good job with <u>McGuffey's Readers</u>, though they came with some humanism. You know you can buy those today. We bought a set. The stories are still there. The teachers don't have to teach them because you are the teacher. Get the <u>McGuffey's Readers</u>, Grades 1-6. Thumb through them. Pick out the stories with great moral truths and principles, right and wrong, good manners, and read those to your children as they're growing up.

Then there are the Aesop fables; great truths there. These are not to take the place of the Bible, but to supplement. These are stories that teach moral truths. And by the way, the Aesop fables are on video now. If you're in luck, watch them on video and see those great truths as they are taught.

Teach your children the Commandments, the "Golden Rule," good manners, honesty and truthfulness. Teach them about life from a Christian perspective.

There is another way you can teach too, and that is by example. I'm afraid children learn more by example than by what we say. You can't tell them not to curse, if you are going to curse in front of them. If you are going to keep alcohol in your home and beer in your refrigerator, you can't do it and tell them not to drink alcohol. You can't tell them not to smoke, if they have been inhaling smoke ever since they were a little baby. You can't tell them not to cheat, if they know mom and dad cheat. You can't tell them not to lie, if they hear you lying to people on the phone in a conversation with other people.

---

[4] There are numerous McGuffey's Eclectic Readers still available today. See <u>McGuffey's Readers</u>, Mott Media (January 4, 1982), ISBN: 978-0880620024

Children are watching and absorbing the life you live before them. They are like wet cement. You leave a great impression on them by what you do and by what you write on their hearts and lives.

Parents Have The Responsibility To Discipline

When children are at the age when they can be impressed by your teaching by example, then discipline is important. Oh, I know discipline is an old-fashioned idea. I know you're not supposed to spank a child anymore. I think the psychiatrists have been leading our young families down the wrong road for far too long. They say, "You don't want to warp their personality. You don't want to warp their little character that wants to play in a can of red paint and splatter the wall."

So, you let them do it because you don't want to warp the personality. Their personality is not what needs to be warped! Children need to know boundaries. They need to know some limitations, and right and wrong.

Suppose you left here today and discovered there's no stop sign in Peachtree City. No stoplights. No speed limit signs. You see what has happened, and the authorities say that while we were in church today, the city council met. Because they love us, and because we are such good citizens, they just took away all the signs and restrictions away.

They said, "Let everybody use their own judgment in driving. Everybody can just drive the way they want to through 54 on the parkway. No stopping, no slowing down, no signal at 74 and 54 coming out of the subdivision. No guidance at all because you don't need it, you are responsible adults. Surely we don't need somebody to enforce laws, rules and regulations. All of us are going to drive responsibly. We all know better. We don't need rules!"

But, we need regulations. Play a game like golf or Monopoly or whatever it is, and you have rules. Play tennis and you have boundary regulations that you follow in order to play the game right.

Children need to know that in life there are "no's." There are stop signs, as well as "go" and "no" and "yes." We tell children, "You can't have candy... well, yes; you can have it after your supper." What is wrong with saying, "No, you can't have candy." Let the child know that there is a "no" in life. Then maybe one day they will say "no" to drugs and "no" to alcohol. There is nothing wrong with teaching them that there are some things they cannot have. You can give them candy after supper if you want to, but you don't always have to meet every need, or want, that they have one way or another in a manipulative way, just so that you do not have to tell them "no."

Discipline. The Bible talks about discipline. Let's just read what the wisest man, who I suppose ever lived, said.

> ***Proverbs 23:13*** Withhold not correction from the child: for *if* thou beatest him with the rod, he shall not die. Thou shalt beat him with the rod, and shalt deliver his soul from hell.

Discipline your child, for in that there is hope. Do not be party to his death!

> ***Proverbs 22:6*** Train up a child in the way he should go: and when he is old, he will not depart from it.

> ***Proverbs 22:15*** Foolishness *is* bound in the heart of a child; *but* the rod of correction shall drive it far from him.

Do not withhold discipline from a child. If you punish him with the rod, he will not die from the rod of correction and wisdom. But, a child left to himself disgraces his mother. That is what the Bible says. It shows us a pattern. The word *discipline* means to disciple or to train. And when the Bible says to train up a child, it recognizes that children need to be trained and taught some guidelines. Here are two or three rules about discipline:

First, be consistent. I failed in that point. I kept moving the sign; moving the boundary sometimes. Sometimes I would be too severe, and at other times, not severe enough. I know better now, and I say that if you can be consistent, then a "no" is a "no," and a "yes" is a "yes." Hold to it as a rule. Abide by that rule and without discussing it. Do not change the rule. Be consistent.

Second, do not be severe. I am not in favor of child beating. I am not a favor of a punishment that leaves a mark! By no means would I advocate that. Do not be severe. That is where we fail a lot in our teaching of parents. It's not the severity of the punishment that is a deterrent. The criminologists tell us this: it is the certainty of it. Capital punishment is not a determent of crime. The determent of crime would be if every criminal knew that if he committed a crime, he would be caught and put on trial, and there would be a punishment.

Whether severe or not, the certainty of punishment is *the* deterrent for your child. Do not be severe. You don't need to be severe. You discipline with your love, your kindness, your firmness, but not too severe.

Third, be consistent so that children will know that if they break the rules, there is a punishment. Far too often we say, "If you do this you will not get to do something else." Then, they do it and they still get to do the something else. We say, "If you don't eat the food on your plate, then you do not get ice cream later." They don't eat the food, and they still get ice cream later. You see, that's not being firm or consistent.

Never humiliate your child. Your child is not stupid or dumb. It really grates on me when I hear people talk about their child saying, "You stupid kid! You dummy!" No! No child is stupid or dumb. It is the parent that is stupid and dumb for calling a child stupid and dumb! Don't humiliate your child! They are tender. They need to build self-esteem. They are somebody! They may do stupid things, but that doesn't make them stupid.

I've done a few stupid things in my life, but I don't think I am stupid. I've done a lot of dumb things in my life, but I don't think I am dumb. Children make mistakes. They do stupid things and dumb things, but they are not stupid and dumb children. They don't need to be told that. They need to be told that they are somebody, and that you love them.

Don't put children down in front of the other kids, or in front of their parents or grandparents, or anyone. Most of all do not ever break your relationship with your child, no matter what happens, no matter what age. Do not break relationships. Do not issue ultimatums. Do not say, "If you do not cut your hair, then you can move out!" Never, never issue an ultimatum to your child; never break your relationship no matter what they do and no matter how far off they are. Keep on loving. Keep the door ajar if they do leave. Help them to know that, even though they rebel and might leave. Older children, now, they rebel, they get angry, and they slam the door! Be careful that *you* do not close the door on them. Let them know that the door will be open when they want to come back home. Do not break that relationship of love.

Parents Have The Responsibility To Love

I can't say enough about love. I don't think I need to say very much about it though, because you know what love is. Parents need to love their children. How do you spell love? T-I-M-E; that is how you spell love! It is not money. It is not things. It is not the most expensive toy, or the most expensive designer jeans. It is not the most expensive shirt. That is not how you spell love. You don't spell love with a new car. You don't spell love with a child getting their own room, or a fancy color TV. That is not how you spell love. Nothing will take the place of you in your child's life. To spell love, spend some time with your child. Devote yourself to your child. Build your life around your child and your child's schedule.

Did you know that that little recital that they are going to give at school or church, or the fact that they are going to stand up and maybe not say a word when they have a little part to sing, this is more important than any ball game that has ever been played in the world. It is more important, even if it is the World Series. It is more important than any golf tournament; it is more important than any club meeting, social gathering, or even a business meeting.

Put your priority in the right place. Be where your child is. Be where your child is and not where the fellows are playing golf, a ball game, or fishing. In those places, your child has a small part. So, let's say someone comes along and offers you a free trip to Hawaii for a week. Say, "I am sorry. I can't go. I have a prior commitment." And, you spend that time with your child.

Birthdays are important. What you do is important. Regulate your life as much as possible around your children.

I know some of you pilots can't call and say, "I am sorry. I can't fly today; it is my son's birthday."

But, the day before, or the day after, or perhaps two days before, you can say, "Son, daughter, I'm going to have to be gone on your birthday, but let's you and I get out there... just the two of us. We'll go have breakfast together and spend a few hours together." Time is important.

What is the reward of a parent? Well, there are a lot of rewards. One is that when you get to heaven, God is going to say, "Well done My good, faithful servant. I sent you a responsibility. I sent you a gift. I sent you a life. I asked you to take that life I love and nurture that child. I asked you to mold that child into a useful person. I asked you to be responsible for the spiritual condition of that child. I sent you a baby a long time ago, and I gave you the responsibility. Now I see that what you have done with that baby. Well done! Well done my good and faithful servant! You've been responsible for this gift I have given you. I am going to make you ruler over many things. You are going to have the love and appreciation of your child."

Your children may think, right now, that you have the meanest parents in the world. Some time ago, I read a story about someone having the meanest mom that ever lived. That mother wouldn't let her teenager do what everybody else was doing. The story ended up with the teenager saying, "Thank You, God! Thank You for letting me have the meanest mom in the world!"

The time will come when your children praise you for standing up and saying, "I love you!" They are going to hug you and kiss you someday when they start their own family. They are going to appreciate what you have done, and they're going to love you. It is going to mean a lot when you appreciate your children.

There's another thing too when it comes to your responsibility to love your children. It is personal joy and satisfaction. There is the joy of seeing your children accept Christ as his Savior! There is the joy of your children selecting their worthy vocation in life. There is the joy of seeing your children selecting their mate and get married. There is the joy of seeing your grandchildren. There is the joy of knowing you didn't break relationships. There is the joy of knowing you built something with the child, and now they want to come home, and they do come home. When they come home, these are the happiest times of the year.

Someone said there are two times when the children come home and we parents are so happy: when their car drives into the driveway; when it drives out! So, you have a double blessing as they come and go, and there is a joy!

I'm going to share something I found some years ago. It is called, "A Child's Ten Commandments To Parents."[5]

1. My hands are small; please don't expect perfection whenever I make a bed, draw a picture, or throw a ball. My legs are short; please slow down so that I can keep up with you.

---

[5] A Child's Ten Commandments To Parents can be found in <u>Parenthood Without Hassles ** Well Almost</u>, Dr. Kevin Leman, Harvest House Pub (June 1979), ISBN 978-0890813041 (the asterisks are part of the book's title)

2. My eyes have not seen the world as you have; please let me explore safely: don't restrict me unnecessarily.
3. Housework will always be there. I'm only little for a short time - please take time to explain things to me about this wonderful world, and do so willingly.
4. My feelings are tender; please be sensitive to my needs; don't nag me all day long. (You wouldn't want to be nagged for your inquisitiveness.) Treat me as you would want to be treated.
5. I am a special gift from God; please treasure me as God intended you to do, holding me accountable for my actions, giving me guidelines to live by, and disciplining me in a loving manner.
6. I need your encouragement, but not your praise, to grow. Please go easy on the criticism; remember, you can criticize the things I do without criticizing me.
7. Please give me the freedom to make decisions concerning myself. Permit me to fail, so that I can learn from my mistakes. Then, someday I'll be prepared to make the kind of decisions life requires of me.
8. Please don't do things over for me. Somehow that makes me feel that my efforts didn't quite measure up to your expectations. I know it's hard, but please don't try to compare me with my brother or sister.
9. Please don't be afraid to leave for a weekend together. Kids needs vacations from their parents, just as parents need vacations from kids. Besides, it's a great way to show us kids that your marriage is very special.
10. Please take me to Sunday school and church regularly, setting a good example for me to follow. I enjoy learning more about God.

Most holy God our heavenly Father, help us to be the kind of parents You would have us to be, and for some of us to be the kind of grandparents You would have us to be. Help us to be the right example, to teach the right things, to give love and discipline when necessary, and to teach Your Word. Go with these parents now, Father. We are so grateful for all the parents here today. We are especially grateful for the mothers on this Mother's Day, who have come to be with their families. How wonderful it is to have a Christian mother, a loving mother, and a mother that wants to be a part of anything the child or grandchild does. And we are grateful for these mothers, who have made a special effort to be here today, for these families that have gathered to worship as families. And, we are grateful for these new babies that have been born into our congregation this past year. Bless each one now as we commit them again to You in Christ's name, Amen.

Dr. Harold and Nancy Allen

Chapter 4: God's Pattern for Parents

CHAPTER 5: WHAT IS THAT IN YOUR HAND?

First Baptist Church, Peachtree City, Georgia
<u>March 26, 1999</u>

"I can't do it."

This is what Exodus tells us that Moses said when God said, "Go down into Egypt and bring the children out of bondage."

"I can't do it," Moses said. "I am slow of speech. If I go down there and tell Pharaoh that God has sent me, he'll laugh me out of the palace. He's not going to believe me. I can't do it. There's no way I can go to Egypt and lead the children out of bondage."

And God said, "Moses, what is that in your hand?"

And Moses said, "Well, it's just a rod, a stick. Every shepherd has one. It's for protection and guidance of the sheep. It's just an old stick."

And God said, "Lay it down. Lay it down, Moses."

And Moses put the stick on the ground and all of a sudden the stick became a snake and began to hiss and slither off.

God said, "Moses, pick it up."

Moses reached down and took the snake by its tail and that snake became an ordinary rod again.

God said, "Moses, you go down to Egypt. You go to Pharaoh and I'll perform the miracles. I'll persuade Pharaoh to let My people go. You just be obedient. You go and I'll do the spectacular through that rod, that stick."

Just an ordinary old stick, but God used it. You know the story. You know how in Egypt, He performed all the miracles that caused Pharaoh to finally yield. You know that when the children of Israel came to the Red Sea, there was no place to go. Pharaoh's army was approaching behind them.

God said, "Take that stick, that rod, and hold it over the Red Sea."

And when Moses did, the sea parted and the children of Israel walked through on dry ground.

And, later, in the middle of the desert when children of Israel were dying of thirst, God said, "Take that stick, that ordinary rod, and hit the rock. Strike the rock and it will bring forth water." And Moses did. The water came gushing forth from the rock. Just an ordinary stick, but God used it as an instrument to do the spectacular, to perform miracles, and to lead the children of Israel out of bondage.

COMMITMENT IS SYMBOLIC

In a few minutes, you are going to take the commitment card that is in your bulletin today. We are going to ask you to make a commitment to our "Forwarding Love" campaign for the next three years. We want a commitment to eliminate, or at least greatly reduce, our debt on the two buildings that God has so graciously allowed us to build.

What's that you hold in your hand? This is the question this morning. The commitment card is just a piece of paper. There is nothing significant about the paper. It is just an ordinary piece of paper with a few words on it. But God says, "Lay it down. Lay it down and I'll use it to bless the multitude. Lay it down and I'll perform the spectacular. Lay it down and I bless the multitude of people." If you are willing to take that commitment as a symbol, then lay it down.

The card is a symbol of what? The commitment card that you have today is an expression of your love for the Lord Jesus Christ and His church.

> ***Ephesians 5:25*** ...as Christ also loved the church, and
> gave himself for it...

God didn't stop at mere words. He went into action. God didn't simply say, "I love you." God sent his Son as an expression of His love. Jesus didn't simply just say, "I love you," He went to the cross and died on the cross because of His great love for you and me. He died that we might have our sins forgiven. He died that we may have meaning and purpose in life. He died that we might have eternal hope to live with our loved ones someday, if we believe in Jesus Christ. He died, and He paid the sacrifice for us.

We come today to express our love for Him. You see, He died to show forth His love. This card is a tangible way that we can say to the Lord Jesus Christ, "I love You." This commitment card gives us an opportunity in a tangible way to express our love.

> *1 John 3:18*   My little children, let us not love in word, neither in tongue; but in deed and in truth.

COMMITMENT INVOLVES ACTION

Ms. Hazel was right when she said that Nancy and I needed to move to Peachtree City.* She doesn't know how right she was. Nancy did not want to come to Peachtree City!

This church did not vote on me as pastor until February 1986. In fact, the pastor's search committee did not even hear me preach until January 1986. I did not accept until the end of February 1986. I came here at the end of March. Let me read from a Christmas card I received in 1985. I've kept it because it means so much to me.

It's says:

> To my husband, I love you. I love you dear, for all you are and everything you do. For dreaming dreams along with me and having them come true. I love you for the happiness you have brought into my life. I love you dear, for you made me the whole world's happiest wife. Merry Christmas. I love you.

I want you to hear what she wrote on the back. She didn't know I was going to do this today. She might be surprised that I still have the card. Here's what she wrote:

> Dearest Harold, Your gift is a little different this year because I couldn't think of anything you wanted or needed, except just one thing. And so I am giving you the only gift I thought you really wanted and something I can't wrap up, but I am giving you my willingness to move to Peachtree City with as little

---

* Ms. Hazel was a close family friend, as well as a member of the congregation, whose opinion was highly valued by the Allen's. Nancy is Dr. Allen's wife.

hassle and as few tears I possibly can. I told you, you could move anywhere you wanted, but I was staying here. But then I remembered years ago, I had promised that where thou goest, I will go and wherever thou lodgest, I will lodge. So I will try and pack and organize and go with a happy spirit, but no one can sell our house here. (*Just so you know, we didn't sell the house for two years after we moved here.*) I know it won't be easy, but I tell you right now I want to go. And, even if there are tears, it doesn't mean I don't want to go. I give you myself. Merry Christmas! (*Italicized* words in parenthesis added by Dr. Allen)

Isn't that great?!

That was her commitment. Yes, it was words, but she put it into action. She did organize, she did pack, and we did move. We had 13 wonderful years, well maybe 11. Eleven out of 13 isn't bad. And, it has been a great, great journey. It's an expression.

OUR COMMITMENT IN ACTION

That is what you are doing today. You are signing a commitment card. In doing so, you are saying "Lord, I love You. I love You for all You've done in my life. I love You for the way You have touched my life. I love You for what You have done in my family. I love You for the way You saved our marriage. I love You for the way You helped our children. Lord, I love the church, because the church has been there for me. It has ministered to me. It has provided for my children. The church has taught me the Word of God. The church has helped me grow, mature, and strengthen my faith. I love the church and I am so grateful the church is there, because in the church I found the Lord. Or, in the church I was baptized. Or, in the church I got married, or in the church I learned more about the Lord Jesus Christ. My children came to the Lord, my children were baptized there. My children got married there. Yes Lord, I love this church and I love You and I want to show it by giving a tangible expression of my love."

Commitment – An Extension of Evangelism

There is something else. The commitment card is an extension of evangelism. That's what we are all about here: reaching the lost. We exist to glorify God by proclaiming the Gospel to the lost. That's why we are here. That's our purpose in being. We believe people are lost outside of Jesus Christ, and we seek to reach them. It is not about building buildings. Never think that! It has nothing to do with building buildings and brick and mortar. That is not what we are about. It's not about budgets. It's about the salvation of lost souls, and if we can do it more effectively through a larger building, *then* we build a building. If we can reach more people through the building and ministry and Sunday school and organization, then we do it! If we can provide a class where a young person can come and receive Jesus Christ, then it is worth every penny it costs to build a building.

If we can provide a preschool where a mother can bring her child to nursery, or to the children's department, and she can know the child is well cared for while she comes to the worship service and hears the gospel of Jesus Christ and comes to know our Savior, then the preschool is worthy.

We are to build more buildings so more people come, and so we can reach more people for Jesus Christ. And as we reach a person, they tell someone else. That person then tells someone else, and the Word continues to spread as more and more people come to know Jesus Christ. It's about reaching out because we believe that sin separates a person from God. We believe that sin can be forgiven through the shed blood of Jesus Christ. We believe that Jesus Christ can give you meaning and purpose to life. He can save you from all the sin, and give you the hope of eternal life; thus, that's why we give. That's why we make commitments. We make commitments because there are people dying without Jesus Christ. Through our commitment, through our giving, we provide the instrument. We provide the rod, we provide the staff, and we provide the means to reach a lost world.

Commitment – Demonstrating Trust And Belief

The commitment card represents even more. The card is a demonstration of your trust and belief in God. It is a demonstration of your faith; faith that God will take care of you, that God will provide.

> ***Luke 6:38*** Give, and it shall be given unto you; good measure, pressed down, and shaken together, and running over, shall men give into your bosom. For with the same measure that ye mete withal it shall be measured to you again.

God says, "Give and I will give to you." Do you believe that? Can you trust God to provide for your needs? Are you more concerned about your 401(k) plan, than the security that God can give you? Do you believe God will provide for you, meet your needs? If so, then give.

We've all raked leaves. We've all tried to put leaves in a garbage bag. We soon filled up the garbage bag, and yet we knew we could get more inside. So, we pushed and pushed and pushed the leaves down. We put in more and more leaves, and then we pushed and pushed. We pressed down and pressed down and put in more leaves. Then, we sat on the bag and got all of the air out of it. We squished it down more and put in more leaves, until we put more leaves in that garbage bag than is humanly possible to put in! It's just impossible to put that many leaves in a bag, but you did it. You kept pressing down, squeezing out the air until you filled it full to the top and the bag was running over.

That's what God is saying. He says that if you give and you are generous in your giving, He will keep blessing you. He will press down and press down and pull together, and press down until you are full and running over with blessings. I believe that! Do you believe it? When you sign the commitment card, it's a demonstration of your trust and belief in God.

> ***Isaiah 30:23*** Then shall he give the rain of thy seed, that thou shalt sow the ground withal; and bread of the increase of the earth, and it shall be fat and plenteous: in that day shall thy cattle feed in large pastures.

God might not bless you materially, but the blessing will always be spiritual. He will bless your family. He will bless your children. Not only is our commitment an extension or expression of our love, it is an extension of evangelism around the world. It is a demonstration of our faith. And, it is also an opportunity to participate in a miracle.

Commitment – Participating In A Miracle

God said to Moses, "You are going down to Egypt, and leave the miracles to Me!"

God used Moses and that staff to perform miracle after miracle. "Lay it down Moses, and I will use it to bless a multitude of people!"

God said, "What's that in your hand? It is My protection! It is My security! I need you."

Moses said, "What's that in my hand? It's my identity! I'm a shepherd! This tells everybody I'm a shepherd. That's who I am, I'm a shepherd!"

So, Moses' security was in that rod. His identity was in that rod, and God said, "Lay it down. Lay it down and I'll bless you."

As you sign that commitment card today, what you are doing is you are laying down your security, a portion of it. And, you are laying down a portion of who you are: your self-worth. In our materialistic world, our security is in our stocks and bonds and lands and what we have materially. That is our security! And many times, who we are is based on what we have. Our self-worth gives us identity.

Still, God said to Moses, "Lay down your security, lay down your self-worth, lay it down. Lay it down and God will perform a miracle."

Today you are going to be asked to come and put your commitment card in this chest as a symbol of your security, as a symbol of your identity. Do this in order that you might participate in a miracle because God is going to perform a miracle here. God already has and is going to perform more in the life of this church. This church is just beginning. The best days are in the future. The greatest is yet to be because of what we are going to do here today. By doing this today, we give God an opportunity to do even greater things in the life of our church. When you fill out that commitment card, lay that card down for the glory of God.

When Moses took that rod, opened up the Red Sea, and the mud dried up, and he got on the other side and looked back, did he say, "Man, look at that! Look at what we did. We came across the Red Sea on dry land. Look what we did." No, Moses and the children of Israel didn't say that. They looked back and when the water was closing on Pharaoh's army, they looked up towards heaven and they said, "Look what He did. To God be the glory." They built an altar. They began to sing praises to God for His greatness, for His majesty, and for what He had done. He had performed a miracle, but they had been able to participate in it. They were a part of it, but God did it. To God be the glory.

A little boy was out one day around the city of Galilee, when the Lord said, "Son, can I have your lunch?"

The boy said, "Well, it's not much. It's just a couple of fishes and five loaves, not much."

Jesus said, "Well, can I have it?"

The little boy gave Him his lunch, he laid it down and you know what happened? Jesus fed the multitude.

And that little boy hurried home. He ran in the house and he said "Mom, dad, you can't believe what I did today! You can't believe what I did today. Today, I took my lunch, I fed 5,000 people! Mom, dad, you can't believe what I did today!"

That's not what he said, no.

I can see him rushing home, "Mom, dad, you won't believe what Jesus did today. You won't believe what He did. He took my meager lunch, He took my ordinary lunch, He took my sardines and biscuits and He fed 5,000 people. You won't believe what Jesus did with that lunch. He multiplied it!"

Folks, it is Jesus that is going to perform the miracle, but I am glad I can bring the lunch. I can bring the biscuits. I can bring the sardines. I can bring a portion and allow Him to take it and multiply and bless multitudes of people, here and around the world. Because what we do is going to keep on serving the Lord until Jesus comes, as we reach out to a lost world in our ministry. The main thing is to reach people for Jesus Christ, and this church intends to always keep the main thing. That's evangelism.

We build buildings and we retire debts, in order that we might keep the main thing the main thing. We call staff and we organize, to keep the main thing the main thing. Reaching the world for Jesus Christ and as we reach them, we train them for Him. This is what commitment for God is all about.

Almighty God and Heavenly Father, we pause here beneath the cross today to say, "We love You, Father." We love Your Son, Jesus Christ, who died for our sins. Today, we've come to put symbols of our appreciation of that love we have for You, to demonstrate our faith and trust in You, and to participate in a miracle that You are going to continue to perform in the life of this church. As You take these gifts and these commitments today, bless them and multiply them and feed and care for the multitude spiritually, Father. So, we pray that You might bless each commitment, and each family that made a commitment. Each person that made a commitment, Father, bless them now, because it represents sacrifice. People have given up some things in order that they might give to You, Father. And we are grateful for their sacrifice, for their commitment, for what You are going to do in their lives as they come to make this type of sacrifice to You. Bless the commitments today, bless the families that have given, bless those who didn't have it to give, Father, but desire to give. Bless each of us now and take these commitments, Father, and use it for Your glory. This is our prayer in Christ's name, Amen.

Jesus and the Thief

CHAPTER 6: THE 7 LAST WORDS

First Baptist Church, Peachtree City, Georgia
<u>March 28, 1999</u>

One's last words are always impressive. We all want to hear the last words of our loved ones. They try to speak, just before they die, and we listen closely and intensely to try and find out what they are saying. We want to take that with us, many times to bring comfort and strength to us, knowing they reflect their last thoughts.

P. T. Barnum's last words were "What are the day's receipts?" You can tell where his life was.

John Quincy Adams said, "The earth is over; I'm content."

Dwight M Moody said, 'Is this death? Well, it's not so bad. In fact, it's glorious. This is my coronation day."

My dad said to me just before he died, "Son, I know heaven is my home."

"I know heaven is my home." My dad knew where he was going. That gives a lot of joy to me. It gave comfort to me, as he gave me his last words to assure me that he knew where he was going. "Son, I know heaven is my home."

Last words are important. I thought it might be useful to look at the last words of our Lord; the last words from the cross. We can go over them in our minds and think about them. Those last words summed up what His life is all about and what His death is all about. They sum up what Jesus came for, and why He lived and died on the cross.

JESUS' LAST WORDS WERE A PRAYER OF FORGIVENESS

As He hung on the cross, there was a jeering crowd, an angry mob. There were soldiers too. They had given so much unjust treatment to Jesus through His trial, or rather mock of a trial. They had beaten Him; they made Him carry his own cross. They put a crown of thorns on His head and they nailed Him to an old cross.

As Jesus looked out from the cross, He began to pray, "Father, Father, Father, forgive them. Forgive them Father for they know not what they do," (Luke 23:34).

Jesus prayed for those who persecuted Him. He prayed for those who cursed Him and jeered at Him. He prayed for those who slapped Him, those who spit on Him, and those who nailed Him to a cross.

He prayed, "Father, Father, forgive them, their spirit is blind. They are ignorant; they don't realize that I am Your son. The whole message hasn't really reached them yet, but Father, forgive each one... this I ask and request. I am dying that they might be forgiven. Father, forgive them."

Jesus started his last words with the word *Father*. He recognized God as his heavenly Father and called Him, "Father." Jesus prayed a prayer of forgiveness. All of Jesus' life was about forgiveness. He was always forgiving, and He taught us to forgive. Over and over He said, "When people mistreat you, you forgive them. When they slap you on one cheek, you turn the other cheek; you forgive them. When they lie about you, when they persecute you, and when they say evil against you; you pray for them and you forgive them."

When Simon Peter became a witness to the Lord (Matthew 18:21-22), he said, "I don't understand all this talk about forgiveness. You keep saying forgive, forgive, and forgive. Is seven times enough? If I forgive my brother seven times, that's all the Law requires. In fact, it's more than the law requires. If I go seven times, that's more than twice what the law requires. I have shown a lot of mercy and a lot of forgiveness, so if I do twice what the law requires, is seven times enough?"

Jesus responded, "Simon, you still haven't understood the message. The message is not about forgiving seven times, but 70 x 7! You keep your little book now, Peter, and when you have forgiven somebody 490 times, I'll think you have done alright."

Jesus was telling Simon Peter, "Live in the spirit of forgiving. You always forgive. You keep on forgiving as long as people need to be forgiven. You don't hold a grudge. You don't strike back. You don't get bitter. You don't get resentful; you forgive. Yes, forgive those who lie about you, those who persecute you, those who undermine you and those who criticize you. You just keep on forgiving."

Jesus' Last Words Were About What We Need

That was Jesus' message from the cross. It was a message for all of us, a message we need. We need His message of forgiveness. Forgive! Jesus didn't give the people what they deserved that day. He gave them what they needed. He gave them forgiveness. Just think, as He hung on the cross and they jeered at Him, cursed Him, laughed at Him, and gambled at the foot of the cross for His garments, Jesus had been unjustly tried, mocked in a trial, and was now on the cross.

If Jesus had not forgiven, we would not have salvation. If He had not forgiven, we would not have the church. If He had not forgiven, we would not have the Bible. If He had not forgiven, we would still be living in our sin, and there would be no hope for us for all eternity. So Jesus didn't give any of us what we deserved, He gave us what we needed.

To that angry mob that day, Jesus said there is enough forgiveness for you too. And on and on, in the great ascension, He prayed this prayer many times… not just one time, but all along the way when He was carrying His cross. He was breathing a prayer, "Father, forgive them." They drove the nails in His hands and He said, "Father, forgive them." When He held the cross and then dropped it, He tore His flesh and He said, "Father, forgive them." Over and over, He was praying for forgiveness. He was teaching us something about how to live life at its best. We are to forgive. Anyone who has hurt us in anyway, we forgive.

You remember, there was a thief on that cross next to Him (Luke 23:39-43). The thief looked over and could not believe what He was hearing. He could not believe what was happening. Here was this man in agony, pain, and dying. Here is this man who had been lied about, ridiculed, and had a spear put in His side. Here was this man hanging on the cross, and rather than curse others or spit on the people below, rather than rebuking them, He was praying. What kind of man was this? What kind of man would pray when people are doing Him an injustice? He was different. Most men curse when they are nailed to the cross. Most men would spit on the people below. But, here was a man who was so different. He was praying. And finally, as that thief listened, he saw the expression on the face of the Lord, and he said to Him,

> *__Luke 23:42__* Lord, remember me when thou comest into thy kingdom.

Notice, the thief didn't say *if* He came to His kingdom. This man was different; he knew where Jesus was going. He said, "Lord, remember me *when* You come into Your kingdom," because he saw something in Christ that was different than any other he had ever known in his whole life. This must be the Messiah. This must be the King of Kings. This must be the One he had heard about. He recognized Christ. He had no scepter in His hand, He had no crown on His head, He had no garments that were royal covering His flesh, but His life, His attitude, and His prayer spoke the truth.

> ***Luke 23:43*** And Jesus said unto him, Verily I say
> unto thee, To day shalt thou be with me in paradise.

Jesus said, Truly, truly, without doubt... you don't have to question it; you can believe it! Jesus didn't say, "Barely, barely, you can believe it is so." Jesus said that before the day was over, the thief and the Lord would be in paradise together.

We too will be in the presence of the Father. Oh, can you imagine, that dying thief in that last hour saying, "Thou forgive us,"? You see, as Jesus prayed for those who persecuted him, the dying thief thought, "There is no pride and there is no sin that is too big for God to forgive." If Christ was willing to forgive those people that had done what they had done to Him, then nothing we have done can be too big for God. He'll forgive us, too.

Nothing you have done is too big for God to forgive, no matter what it is. Just as He forgave those who persecuted Him, He will forgive us. And the thief must have sensed that. He thought that no matter how rotten his life had been, no matter how many people he had robbed, and no matter how many people he had beaten or killed, this man on the cross could forgive him, and will forgive him. He knew this because He forgave those who nailed Him to a tree and who were killing him.

Jesus prayed that prayer. I can see the end of the day. Jesus is on His way back home. And, we must not forget to remember one other person too, because under His arm was that dying thief. They were walking to heaven together. Those in heaven looked out and they said, "Hey there, He's coming, the Son is coming, the Son is coming. Jesus is on His way back, but who is that with Him?" He is not alone, and they look again. "Well, that's... that thief who was on the cross next Him! He is bringing a thief into heaven." And they walked into heaven together, because that day they entered paradise together.

And then, our Lord looked down on that sea of hatred and bitterness. He looked on that sea of rejection and on that sea of animosity, and there was a little island of love. There stood His mother. He looked down at His mother and He said, "Woman, behold thy son," as He looked toward John. He said, "John, behold thy mother," (John 19:26-27), as He looked at Mary.

The word *woman* that Jesus used refers to a woman of endearment; it is a word of respect. It is not like the way we would use the word *woman* today, for example, "Women do this, or women do that." He was saying, "My dearly beloved, the one I respect, the one I love, woman, behold thy son."

On that day, as Jesus was dying, He thought about his mother and He wanted to make sure His mother was taken care of. Honor thy father and mother. He was honoring the earthly mother, who had raised Him and who had given birth to Him. He was saying, "I want you to be cared for."

Why didn't Jesus give his mother to be under the care of one of her brothers? It is because they weren't there; they had rejected Him. Maybe they thought He had lost His mind, or that He was crazy. They had come, but they had tried to get Him to go home. They had given up on Jesus, but a mother never gives up. A mother keeps on loving. That's a true mother.

As she made her way right to the foot of the cross to stand there, she was looking up and she saw His lips move. It was then that He called out, "Woman, behold thy son." And He gave to John a tremendous responsibility. "John, you take My mother, you care for her, and you meet her needs. I trust you John; you have been My faithful disciple. You have been the beloved one, and I know you have enough love in your heart to take care of Mary."

I think the Lord was saying something else that day too. He was saying, "Mary, as close as I am to you, as much as I love you, as much as you love Me, I am no longer your son, today I am your Savior. And, John is going to become your son. You'll adopt him, and you'll take care of him because you cannot worship Me as your son. From now on, you must worship Me as your Savior, as the One Who died on the cross for your sins."

So, Jesus was teaching her. She had no special blessings with God the Father, except through faith in Him and His atoning death on the cross. She broke the cord that day; or rather, He broke the cord that day. He turned over to John that responsibility.

Christ prayed that prayer, which we can't understand, "My God, My God, My God, why have You forsaken Me? My God, why, why have You forsaken Me?!"

Martin Luther looked at that prayer. He pondered that prayer, and he spent hours meditating on that prayer, that that word from the cross. Finally, he got up and said, "Who can understand God forsaking God? No one can. It is beyond our understanding that God would forsake His own Son."

Martin Luther was never able to reconcile that crime on the cross. "My God, My God, why has thoust forsaken me?"

It is difficult to understand, unless you realize what took place on the cross. In those three hours that Jesus hung on the cross, He was taking your sin and my sin upon Himself. He took all of our sin.

Can you imagine the sin in your own life? Just take the sin, all that you committed, all your life, and put it in a cup. What happens when a cup of bitter poison pours into man? Take your sin and multiply it by a million, multiply it by 10 million for all the sins of the whole world, and put it into that bitter cup, and then put all of it upon Jesus Christ. He had all our sins on Him, in Him, around Him, and so God turned His back. It was nauseating even to God because the sin was so great. Jesus, as He died with all of our sins, took your penalty and my penalty.

I believe the scholars are right. I believe that in that period of time, when Jesus felt forsaken, He went to hell and He experienced all of the pain, agony, and suffering and pain Himself, being in a place where God wasn't. You see, I think that the greatest punishment after death, if you don't have Jesus Christ as Savior, is that you will be forever departed from God. You will never know God, if you die without Jesus Christ in your heart. You will go to eternity in hell. For all eternity, you will be in no fellowship with God the Father.

When Jesus took our punishment, when Jesus took our sin, God turned His back. *Forsaken* is a terrible word. It is terrible for a husband to forsake his wife; for a parent to forsake a child; for children to forsake the parent. It's a terrible thing to be forsaken. To be forsaken by a friend is a horrible thing. But to be forsaken by God, nothing can be worse than that. And yet, Jesus Christ, because He loves you and me, endured separation from God the Father. He endured the agony of pain and hell Himself. "My God, My God, why have You forsaken Me?" He knew the answer. He knew that because He had our sin upon Himself, voluntarily, willingly, and vicariously, He had to die.

Christ took our place. He took the forsaking of God for Himself. And after that, of course, there was a period of time, a little over three hours, before He finished His last words. It was then that He said, "I thirst." Notice, He never thought about His own need until He had already gone to the pits of hell for you and me. He thought about those who had persecuted and crucified Him. He prayed for forgiveness. He thought about the people while on the cross, and He promised them salvation, a prayer, and a word of salvation. He thought about His mother. He took care of His mother. And then, He went into the pits of hell for all of us, dying for our sins. Afterwards He said, "I thirst." He experienced agony, without water, and having the need for water. He was thirsty. This tells us something about what He went through to give us eternal life.

All the liquids went out of His body. They tell me that thirst is one of the most tormenting of all forms of suffering; to crave a drink… to crave water, and not be able to get any water.

Sometimes, when people have surgery, they can't drink water for an hour to two, or maybe a day or two after surgery. They cry out for some water. You dampen a cloth and touch it to their lips, because they want some moisture there. Their body is crying out for some fluids and some liquids. They need it, and they are in pain without it.

Jesus Christ hung on that cross between heaven and earth. The sunrays were taking the fluids out of His body. He had a crown of thorns on His head. He had had the whip on His back. He had the spear thrust in His side, and all that blood had left His body. All that fluid left His body, and there He was hanging and needing something to moisten His lips, just one drop of water.

It reminds me of the rich man, Lazarus. The rich man went to hell and cried for one drop of water. Jesus Christ went to hell for you and me. He came out with parched lips and a desire for a drink of water, our thirst.

JESUS' LAST WORDS WERE ABOUT COMPLETION

After Jesus had endured, He said one word. He said, "Finished." In the Greek, it is translated as, "It is finished." What was finished? Well, Jesus had finished His mission. He had accomplished His mission. He had finished the work of salvation. He had finished our redemption. He had finished God's plan, that we might be saved.

You see, when man sinned against God in the Garden of Eden, the sin built a barrier, a wall between man and God. Man tried to get across that barrier. Man tried to build a bridge back to God in different ways. But, God made a sacrificial system, and through that sacrificial system, man could have access to God. There was the sacrifice of animals, and there was a holy place: the Holy of Holy's. There the lambs were sacrificed for sin, according to how God put this sacrificial system in place. Sinful man could come into the presence of a Holy and righteous God, but still God was kind of off limits in the sense that a person had to go through the sacrificial system of bringing the lambs.

When Jesus Christ died on the cross, He opened up the Holy Ghost to all of us. Jesus became the lamb, the sacrifice for your sin and my sin, so that we never have to offer another lamb up for our sins. He said the plan of salvation is finished... with nothing to add to it. God was in Christ, and He reconciled this world to Himself.

So, what was finished? Our relationship with God the Father had been restored, and we could come back into fellowship with God, the fellowship that Adam lost in the Garden of Eden. Because Adam was the "head" of the human race, we all were lost, that is until Jesus brought it back on the cross.

Jesus had finished what He came to earth to do. He came to seek and save sinners. He came to make a way where sinners could go and live for all eternity with the Holy Father in heaven. "It is finished." He was saying, "Father, I have done what You asked Me to do. I have finished My mission on earth. I have completed the plan of salvation. No one can ever add to it or take away from it."

He finished it, and it is perfect. He looked back towards heaven and He said, "Father, into Thy hands, I commend My spirit." In other words, "Father, I am ready to come home now." He started his last words with, "Father, forgive them." He finished His last words with, "Father, I am ready to come home." He never lost the fact that God was the Father, and I believe even when He was crying out "My God, My God," He still knew the God He was crying out to was His Father. He started and ended by recognizing God as His Father. He passed the test. "Father, I commit Myself now totally to You. I have committed My life, I have fulfilled My mission, and I am ready to come home."

I trust that when we come to the end of our journey, when life is over, we pray that prayer as our last prayer, as Jesus had it as the last prayer on His lips, "Father, I'm ready, I commend my spirit to You. Father, I'm ready to come home." Jesus went on to meet the Father, along with the dying thief.

That is what it is all about folks. It is not how wealthy we become, how secure we have become in this world, or how much fame, recognition, or popularity we get. What is really going to count, when we come to the end of life, is that we know we have the will of the Father. What will count is that we are ready to release ourselves back to Him, without a struggle, without a fight, simply saying, "Lord, I am ready now, my life is over, thank You for the good life I had, now I am coming home."

JESUS' LAST WORDS WERE ABOUT LOVE

What does all this mean? It simply means that God loves you very much. God loves me very much. Jesus went to the cross and died on it because of His great love for you and me.

> ***Romans 5:8*** But God commendeth his love toward us, in that, while we were yet sinners, Christ died for us.

That's what it is all about. That is what the cross says, "God loves you. God loves you. God loves you. God loves you, with an everlasting love."

> ***John 3:16*** For God so loved the world, that he gave his only begotten Son, that whosoever believeth in him should not perish, but have everlasting life.

When I see the cross, I know that God loves me. It tells me I have worth in the sight of God, because God died for me, as if I was the only person in the whole world. He saw enough in me that He was willing to go to the cross and pay for my redemption. God loves me, and I have worth to God. I may not have worth to anybody else in this whole universe, but I am somebody to God. I know because His Son went to the cross to redeem me, to save me, and to secure for me a place in heaven someday.

There was a priest in the Middle Ages, and he announced he was going to preach a sermon on the love of God. A priest in the Middle Ages didn't preach many sermons. They didn't have great cathedrals or places of worship that were lit up. When the people gathered, they packed the chapel that day, to hear the priest preach that sermon on the love of God. They were anxious to hear what he was going to say.

Well, they came in and there was just one candle out front; no other lights in the cathedral. They took their seats and waited. The time came, and the priest went over and took the candle out of the candle holder. He walked up to the cross and held it at the feet of Jesus, the crucifix. He held it for a little while, so they could really get the picture. The priest climbed on a little stool and went up and held the candle first at one side at one hand and then the other side at the other hand. Then, he reached a little higher, he climbed a little higher and he held the light right at the crown of thorns on the head of Christ. There was the crucifix. Finally, he climbed down, he turned and he walked out. People wondered what happened, but the service was over. The sermon was finished. He had preached his sermon on the love of God without saying a word; all he did was point to the cross.

God loves you and the cross says far more than I could ever say: Christ died for each of us.

CHAPTER 7: TODAY'S CHILD – TOMORROW'S HOPE

First Baptist Church, Peachtree City, Georgia
May 9, 1999

The world says the family is a democracy. The world says that you get together and you decide together, because even children should have equal input. But, the Bible says,

> ***Colossians 3:20*** Children, obey *your* parents in all things: for this is well pleasing unto the Lord.

Children are to be submissive to their parents. Children don't have a vote in the bathroom. They are just children, they are babies, and they are your responsibility as parents. Children don't have the maturity to have a vote in any decision. You might ask their opinion, but you, mom and dad, make the decisions. Children are to obey the parents.

The world says you don't spank because that brings violence. That is wrong. The Bible says,

> ***Proverbs 23:13*** Withhold not correction from the child: for *if* thou beatest him with the rod, he shall not die. Thou shalt beat him with the rod, and shalt deliver his soul from hell.

Bible says to discipline your child. The world says you shouldn't have gender distinction. The world says that little girls should play with little boys' things. The world says that little boys should play with little girls' things. The world says to make no distinction. The Bible says,

> ***Genesis 1:27*** So God created man in his *own* image, in the image of God created he him; male and female created he them.

71

The Bible says boys and girls children are different. There is a distinction.

The world says that the goal is to give children self-esteem, to help them feel important, to build them up. The Bible says,

> **_1 Peter 5:5_** …for God resisteth the proud, and giveth grace to the humble.

So you see, as parents you've got to decide where you are going to go. Are you going to go to the world to get your answers, or are you going to go to the Word of God?

Thomas Sowell wrote an article in the newspaper this past week.[*] You know there is a lot of talk about suing parents now for the actions of their children? He says that of all the rational ideas thrown around in the wake of the high school shooting in Middleton, Colorado; one of the most reckless is the proposal to hold parents legally responsible for what children do.[**] Responsibility and control go together.

For decades, our laws and educational system have consistently undermined parental authority. Yet, new legal responsibilities for parents are being proposed, even though parental control has already been eroded. Preschoolers are being taught that their parents have no right to spank them. All sorts of propaganda programs are in the schools, from the so-called, "Drug Prevention" to "Sex Education." These programs stress that each individual should be able to make his or her own decisions, independently of parental or godly values.

The newspaper article says that handing out condoms at school, and giving girls abortions behind parents' backs, are not just isolated manifestations of this underlining philosophy, which reaches far beyond sexual matters. There are nationwide networks that have distributed prepackaged programs designed to bring school children away from the values from which they have been raised. These programs mold children to the value of being self-anointed agents of

---

[*] Thomas Sowell is a columnist from the Hoover Institute, who contributes articles to a number of different newspapers, and has written a number of books on a variety of subjects. He often contributed to the <u>Atlanta Small Business Monthly</u>, which Dr. Allen often read.

[**] Dr. Allen is referring to the Columbine Massacre that happened a couple weeks prior to this sermon, on April 20, 1999. The killings took place in Littleton, Colorado.

change. Invasions of family privacy in children's daily homework assignments and instructions are all part of the same mindset.

Similar groups like the so-called, "Children's Defense Fund," seeks legal power to impose their notions on how children should be raised. Hillary Clinton's "pious hokum," that it takes a village to raise a child, is more of the same.

The article goes on to say much more. Running through each of these programs is the notion that morality is optional. If it feels good, do it. We will never know how good it felt to those young killers to shoot down those around him, nor can we know how much the school's own reckless experiment in brainwashing contributed to the tragedy.

It is truly daunting to have those who would undermine the morality of parents to now demand that parents become legally responsible for the acts of their children.

We've listened to the legal side and to the liberals. We've listened to the experts. We've done what they have said, and we have chaos in light of it. The social experiment of the 60's and 70's has failed, totally. Do the math and figure it out. They are wrong. They just don't want to accept responsibility for it. And now that they are proven wrong, they have come back to say that the parents are legally responsible. It is as if we have taken control from the parents. Over and over, the experts said, "We know how to raise your child. We can do a better job. You have no input; you have no say. You can't correct your children."

Who are we going to listen to? I choose to listen to the Word of God.

> ***Proverbs 22:6*** Train up a child in the way he should
> go: and when he is old, he will not depart from it.

What does this tell us?

CHILDREN CAN BE TRAINED

It tells us that children can be trained. They can be motivated. They can be guided. They can be developed in the right direction.

When we built our concrete driveway, our little dog, Edelweiss, who weighs 4 lbs., walked on the wet cement and left little paw prints across it. The concrete was wet; it was pliable. The weight made an impression on that wet cement. Today, an elephant walking across it couldn't make an imprint.

Children are like wet cement. They are impressionable. They absorb what takes place in the home. Prints are made on their minds that last their whole lives. It affects who they are going to become later in life. If there is anger, bickering, hostility, cursing, or arguing in the home, it makes an impression. If there is love, kindness, forgiveness, and prayer, it also makes an impression. It's what you do in the home that makes a difference.

As someone has written,

> I took a piece of plastic clay,
> And idly fashioned it one day.
>
> And as my fingers pressed it still,
> It moved and yielded at my will.
>
> I came again when the days were passed,
> The bit of clay was hard at last.
>
> The form I gave it still it bore,
> But I could change that form no more.
>
> I took a piece of living clay,
> And gently formed it day by day.
>
> And molded with my power and art,
> A young child's soft and yielding heart.
>
> I came again when days were gone,
> It was a man I looked upon.
>
> That early impress still he wore,
> And I could change it, never more.[6]

People come to me and say, "I cannot do anything with my teenager. What's wrong?"

I'm sad to say it's too late. It's too late, apart from the intervention of God, because the impressions have already been formed, and they

---

[6] *A Piece of Plastic Clay*, Author Unknown

are set. As concrete is set up, by the time a child is five years old, 75% of his character and personality is already formed.

Who is going to teach your child in his early years? Is it the TV? Are you so busy that you put them in front of the TV? Do you put them with a TV in the room and let them watch?

Their little minds! If it is a Walt Disney movie that they watch, realize that Walt Disney is doing more to damage our kids' minds than any other family program out today. Their little character cartoons are full of mistakes, which undermine the Bible's teaching. They are teaching a philosophy that is totally contrary to the Word of God. Watch what your kids are watching.

Daycare workers are going to form your child's attitude, personality, and character in years to come... is that important? Listen to your child and train your child, because you can mold your child.

You might ask the question, "How? How do we train our children?" Number one is discipline.

DISCIPLINE IS VITAL TO TRAINING

> ***Proverbs 19:18*** Chasten thy son while there is hope,
> and let not thy soul spare for his crying.

I had two boys. My oldest boy was kind of defiant in high school, and I could rebuke him and spank him, which I did and he refused to cry. He just would not.

My youngest son walked in the door crying when he had done something wrong. He was so remorseful, so sorry... all those tears. Sometimes I made the mistake of looking at those tears and thinking they were genuine, when they were really false repentance. That is all it was. My youngest didn't want me to spank him. Don't worry about the tears, the false repentance.

> ***Proverbs 22:15*** Foolishness *is* bound in the heart of a
> child; *but* the rod of correction shall drive it far from
> him.

Dr. Spock taught us that children are like little angels, who just have to be loved and cared for, in order to bring the good out of the child. That's not what the Bible teaches. The Bible says the man has a dark side. We all have a dark side. We are not *angels* who have to be loved individually. We are little devils. We have to correct the little devil that is within us.

Who is it that's bound up in the heart of a child? The heart is where we come from, it's our true heart. Children are precious, that's why they are beautiful and lovable. But, inside that child is a heart that's bent towards evil… it's the sin nature.

Mark Twain said, "Man is like the moon, it has a dark side." The Bible goes on to say,

> ***Proverbs 23:13*** Withhold not correction from the child: for *if* thou beatest him with the rod, he shall not die. Thou shalt beat him with the rod, and shalt deliver his soul from hell.

You have to decide, are you going to listen to the Word of God or are you going to listen to the people of the world?

In the April 1999 <u>Atlanta Small Business Monthly</u>, I noticed an article written by a business woman. She is not a preacher, not a counselor, not a teacher, but a lady who is in the business world. She wrote, "I read some excerpts from a book written by the man who was a lead expert on child rearing, long before Dr. Spock. There was an entire chapter on how kissing and hugging your children would make them weak and dependent. It says only to kiss them on the forehead before bed, if you absolutely can't restrain yourself."

I guess that explains the sour faces on old photographs! As a parent, I couldn't get that article out of my head. Sure, we know the book she was talking about is ridiculous, but at the time that book was written and viewed as presenting cold hard facts. People were blindly accepting it simply because the "experts" said to. Personally, I believe in years to come we will look back on the current "You Shall Never Spank Your Children Theory" and discover that it is much the same kind of bull. I believe it presents a lack of serious discipline that has, at least in part, led to the moral decline we've experienced in this nation.

We now have a generation of kids who have slapped their parents, stayed out all night, had sex by the age of 12. They basically do whatever they want… in spite of parental objections. We have school bus drivers who get beat up by kids, and 10 year old children of whom teachers are afraid. We keep lowering the age where we try children as adults. At younger and younger ages, children commit serious adult offenses. Teenage pregnancies and drug and alcohol abuse are major problems. All of this cuts across economic lines.

This change has occurred since we have moved away from the paddle in favor of the "Let's Talk It Over" approach. Do the math. I have never met a well-behaved, respectful child who didn't experience the occasional spanking. Time-outs and talking it over had its place, but for serious infractions I think you need serious punishment, so that they learn that actions of real consequences... sometimes deserve serious consequences.

My father spanked me only occasionally, but when he did, it hurt. I don't feel abused. I realize now that those spankings really had hurt him more than they hurt me. It taught me that if I crossed a certain line it was going to be painful, literally. The fear kept me from doing things I would have liked to have tried, things that I am now grateful I was too afraid to attempt. I listened to my parents mostly because I respected them, but partly because I feared the repercussions of disobeying. It's a lesson that has helped me make better decisions as an adult. As a child I received far more hugs than spankings, but I thank God that when it was occasionally needed, my parents had the discipline to dole out the hard punishment too.

The Atlanta Small Business Monthly article goes on to tie the issue of discipline to today's companies and employers, and how they need to get back to discipline in the work place. It's really an article written to the CEOs of companies. It parallels what's happening in the work place with what's happening at home, and how the work place has some of the same problems as home.

> Jim Garner, are you here this morning?*** Where are you? Come up here.
>
> Jim is so violent. He is a violent person. You ought to see him sometimes. He gets so angry, so upset, so violent, he just hits people all the time. And, I guess that's because his mother spanked him when he was growing up. Is that right?
>
> He's not buying it. Jim is one of the meekest, tender hearted, best guys I know. Give him a round of applause.

*** Jim Garner was the Youth Pastor at Peachtree City Baptist at the time of this sermon. Basically, Dr. Allen was calling upon him as an example. Their spiritual-family relationship was such that this impromptu "object lesson" was necessary, valuable, and perfectly OK.

This week I was talking to Jim in the office and I just patted him on the back and said, "Jim, you are doing a great job. I appreciate what you are doing with the youth."

The sermon was on my mind, and I said something to Jim about spanking. I said, "Of course you don't know anything about spanking because you never did anything wrong." Surely through his whole life, even now, he's never done anything wrong!

I said, "You don't know anything about spanking because I know your mother never spanked you."

He replied, "Yes, she did."

I said, "You're kidding!"

He said, "There is a yellow ruler that is still hanging in the house." Even though his mother passed away, the ruler is still there as a reminder.

I asked, "Why in the world did she spank you?"

He said, "Sometimes I was disobedient and I needed it."

Jim turned out pretty good, didn't he? I tell you, he's alright.

This idea that spanking creates problem-children is a bunch of malarkey. Its bull is what it is. I grew up in a generation of spanking and our generation isn't going out and shooting, and, as students and kids, we weren't beating up teachers.

I am glad we got a Youth Director like Jim, who was spanked few times.

George Beverly Shea was asked, "Were you ever spanked?"

He said, "Well, in our kitchen there was a razor strap on the wall. It was hung next to a plaque that said, 'I need thee every hour.'"

So, maybe that's the ruler Jim had in his mother's kitchen. A yellow ruler... he even knew the color. "I need thee every hour," especially when we are disobedient. Discipline, it is so important. It is important to teaching your children the Word of God.

TEACHING THE WORD OF GOD IS PART OF TRAINING

> ***Deuteronomy 6:4-9*** Hear, O Israel: The LORD our God *is* one LORD: And thou shalt love the LORD thy God with all thine heart, and with all thy soul, and with all thy might. And these words, which I command thee this day, shall be in thine heart: And thou shalt teach them diligently unto thy children, and

shalt talk of them when thou sittest in thine house, and when thou walkest by the way, and when thou liest down, and when thou risest up. And thou shalt bind them for a sign upon thine hand, and they shall be as frontlets between thine eyes. And thou shalt write them upon the posts of thy house, and on thy gates.

Teach your children the Bible's commandments. Teach right and wrong from God's Word. Teach your children what God has to say. Build a foundation for your child.

I say to young parents, "Start now." Tell your children Bible stories and bring them to church. On your way to church, build a foundation. Build a love for God by teaching them the Word of God. Teach them what's important, about what really counts. How do you train a child? You train a child by how you live and how you walk.

I seldom quote Dr. Spock. Perhaps you know he was opposed to spanking children. He said that spanking was wrong, until he married a lady who had a couple of children. Dr. Spock came to recant what he said earlier in his book. You have to get a child's attention before you talk to him. Dr. Spock figured that out.

Dr. Spock did say on one occasion, "The best upbringing children can receive is to observe their parents taking basic care of themselves, mind, body and spirit." Children have been the world's greatest mimics; naturally and automatically they model their parents' behavior. They grow up to be like us in spite of all our mistakes. We need a better generation of parents if our kids are to be tomorrow's hope. We need to change some things in our lives.

Someone said,

> You know we read in the papers
> And we hear on the air
> Of killing and stealing
> And crime everywhere.
>
> And we sigh and we say
> As we notice the trend,
> This young generation
> Where will it end?
>
> But can we be sure
> That it's their fault alone,

I mean, that maybe a
Part of it isn't our own!

Are we less guilty
Who place in their way
Too many things
That lead them astray?

Like too much money to spend
And too much idle time,
Too many movies
The kind of passion and crime.

Too many books, man
That are not even fit to be read,
Too much evil in what they hear said,

And too many children
Encouraged to roam
By too many parents
Who won't even stay at home.

Well, man, kids don't make the movies
And they don't write the books
And they don't go out
And paint gay pictures
Of gangsters and crooks.

They don't make the liquor
And they don't run the bars
And they don't make the laws
And they don't buy the cars.

They don't peddle junk that
Well, that addles the brain,
That's all done by older folks, man
Greedy for gain.

When Delinquent teenagers come home, oh, man
How quick we do condemn
The sins of a nation
And then go and blame it on them.

> But the laws that are blameless
> The Savior makes known
> Now you tell me who is there among us
> To cast the first stone?
>
> For in so many cases
> It's sad but it's true,
> That the title, "Delinquent"
> Fits older folks too.[7]

We must not be delinquent parents. We have to set an example. How do you train your kids? You train them through discipline, through teaching, and through example, but in which way? We train them "in the way they should go." We train them upwards, towards God spiritually.

What's the goal you have for your child... to be popular? Is the goal to be happy? I hope not. Those are all secondary.

> *Matthew 6:33* But seek ye first the kingdom of God, and his righteousness; and all these things shall be added unto you.

The goal you should have for your child is for your child to come to know Jesus Christ, to have a relationship with God the Father. That's your number one goal. It's more important than being successful and popular, even happy.

Somewhere along the line, teach your child to respect God. Then, you teach your child outward, socially, how to act. Teach your child how to interact, how to be kind, to be giving, to be loving, and to be sharing. You teach your child how to live in the world, how to be free of prejudice, how not to look down on people, how not to criticize people, and how not to make fun of people.

Part of the problem in Colorado was the fact that the kids were different. That shouldn't have been a problem, but because they were different, people shunned them, people ignored them, people criticized them, people laughed at them, and people made jokes about them. And so, hatred built and built and built. Teach your children not to make fun, or to have prejudice or hatred towards anybody, any race, or any

---

[7] These are the lyrics from Sammy Davis, Jr.'s song, *Don't Blame it on the Children.* This song can be heard on YouTube!

color. Free yourself of that prejudice. Teach your children how to live in a world that is multi-colored and multi-cultured, a world that has different economic levels. Teach them how to respect people as people, not for what they have.

Quit building your child's ego, self-esteem, and worth by what he wears. It doesn't make any difference what we wear. It's what's on the inside that counts. We've got to get that across. You may make a salary 10 times what I make, but that doesn't make you any smarter, better or any closer to God than I am, or any more important either. It doesn't make your word count any more than the word of a custodian in the church.

I don't know where we get this idea that our worth is wrapped up in what we make, what we wear, what we drive, or where we live. Teach your children to see people as people, not as a reflection or an extension of their parents.

Socially, and then inwardly, build character. Regardless of what the spin-doctors say, character does matter. Teach your child truth, integrity, honesty, right and wrong. Character does matter, it is important. Don't think, "It doesn't matter or affect my child," oh yes it does! Character, or lack of it, affects all of one's relationships and decisions through one's life.

You do these things and your child will be blessed. Your child will not forget what you teach. Plant the seed when your child is a baby. Even before they are born, you must be in the process of planting the seed. You must plant that seed for five years, for 10 years... it may lay dormant for a while. Because of peer pressure and other pressures, your children may forget and go astray, but the seed will still be there.

Through prayers and tears, through your watering and your concern, the seed will sprout again and start to grow. Down the road, that child will remember what he learned as a child. That man, that woman, will remember, and like the prodigal child, they will come home. "Father, I know I've sinned." How do they know they've sinned? They will know because you taught them right from wrong. If you didn't teach your child right from wrong, then he won't know right from wrong. He won't know what he should do from what he could get away with. You teach your children, and when they are old they will not depart from it.

It takes a parent to raise a godly child. Help us Father. In Your will, with your love and care we pray, in Christ's name, Amen.

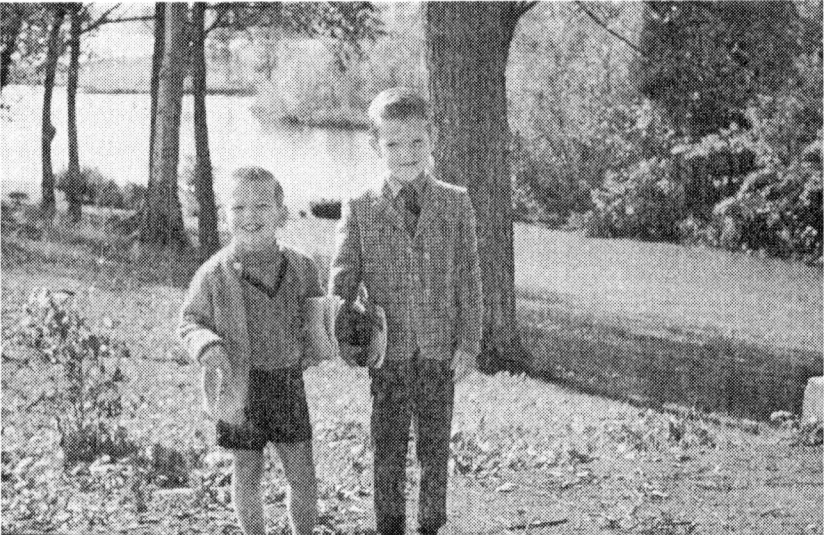

Stephen and David Allen

Chapter 7: Today's Child – Tomorrow's Hope

CHAPTER 8: TO SPANK OR NOT TO SPANK

First Baptist Church, Peachtree City, Georgia
<u>May 23, 1999</u>

Hebrews 12:4-11 Ye have not yet resisted unto blood, striving against sin. And ye have forgotten the exhortation which speaketh unto you as unto children, My son, despise not thou the chastening of the Lord, nor faint when thou art rebuked of him: For whom the Lord loveth he chasteneth, and scourgeth every son whom he receiveth. If ye endure chastening, God dealeth with you as with sons; for what son is he whom the father chasteneth not? But if ye be without chastisement, whereof all are partakers, then are ye bastards, and not sons. Furthermore we have had fathers of our flesh which corrected *us*, and we gave *them* reverence: shall we not much rather be in subjection unto the Father of spirits, and live? For they verily for a few days chastened *us* after their own pleasure; but he for *our* profit, that *we* might be partakers of his holiness. Now no chastening for the present seemeth to be joyous, but grievous: nevertheless afterward it yieldeth the peaceable fruit of righteousness unto them which are exercised thereby.

I am told that a pilot in a small plane can become so jostled about by wind and storm that he can develop a case of vertigo. He can lose his equilibrium, and cannot tell if the plane is upside down or not. He cannot tell which way the plane is going, whether it is going up or down! The pilot can lose all sense of direction, and if he does not look to the instrument panel, he can fly the plane to the ground or into a mountain, and crash the plane. So, he must not fly by the seat-of-his-pants. He must not fly by his emotions or by what he thinks is best, but by the instrument panel, if he is to bring the plane to a safe landing.

I believe parents today have been so jostled about by philosophies, by the views of a liberal media, and by so-called "experts," that they've lost their spiritual equilibrium. They don't know how to be parents. They are struggling. They've lost all sense of direction because everyone is saying something different. "Do this, do that, do something else, or try this." Parents don't have any sense of what's right and what's wrong, what's best.

So I say to you, as parents, if you are to raise your children and bring them through life safely, you must rely on the instrument panel, which is God's Word. You must come back to the sound advice that God has given over the years to His people on how to raise children. We must come back to what God implants within us, as parents, when we have children. God gives us intuition on how to raise that child. He gives us guidance from His Word, and also from our feelings. We should depend on them, and not the so called "experts" all around us.

A book, John Rosemond's <u>Six-Point Plan for Raising Happy, Healthy Children</u> is a tremendous book.[8] I liked it because he is not a preacher, he is not theologian, but he's a Ph.D. in child psychology. He has taken all the courses in how to raise children, how to react to children, and he understands the academic approach to child rearing. In the introduction to this book, he says,

> "During our first few years of parenthood, my wife, Willie and I read all the right books and did all the supposedly right things, those supposed experts advised. (*Because he was one of the experts.*) But, everything went wrong anyway. They said to respect Eric as an equal, but the more respect we showed him, the less he showed us. They said family should be democratic, but the more democratic we were the more of a tyrant Eric became. They said it was wrong to control children, but the less control we exercised the more out of control he was. The more wrong things went, the more guilt we felt, the more insecure Eric was and the more crazy we all were. In time, we

---

[8] <u>Six-Point Plan for Raising Happy, Healthy Children</u>, John Rosemond, Andrews McMeel Publishing, 1989, ISBN: 978-0836228069

discovered that the more child bearing books we read, the more we believed that experts had the answers, the more we lost touch and trust with ourselves. And so about 3 years into the game, we stopped listening to the experts and began raising Eric, not by the book, but by the heart. In that 4th year of Eric's life, the 1st year of Amy's, Willie and I took our first step towards becoming experts at raising children. My one purpose of writing this book is to put you, the reader, in touch with your capacity of being an expert at raising your children. I want to put you back in touch with common sense. I want you to understand that while raising children is not always fun, it does not have to be difficult and it can always be rewarding. In short, I want you to learn to depend on yourself and raise your children."[9] (*Italicized* words in parenthesis added by Dr. Allen)

The point that he talks about is common sense. John Rosemond has written another book too, Parent Power.[10] He is recognized as one of the experts today in child rearing. He has received many awards, has been on many programs, and has written many books. In fact, he has a column in the newspaper. Most importantly, the common sense approach he is talking about is all found right here in God's word, although he doesn't say that.

I don't know if John Rosemond is a Christian or not, but the way we have been raising children in the past was based on the Word of God, and he calls that common sense. I call that spiritual sense. I call it Biblical sense, and going back to the Word of God.

VIOLENCE AND SPANKING

I want to talk about something that we have really been told is wrong, and that is spanking. We've been told, "Oh, that's the worst thing you can do to a child. You teach a child to hit, and you teach a

[9] ibid.
[10] Parent Power, John Rosemond, Andrews McMeel Publishing; Original edition (January 1, 1991) , ISBN: 978-0836228083

child to resolve all of his conflict by hitting." That's what they say, "Violence breeds violence."

Many surveys and studies have been done on violence compared to spanking. There is absolutely no correlation between spanking and violence. The correlation is "point zero, zero (.00)" between spanking and violence. And yet, the experts still try to teach that we must not touch a child. We can be arrested in America if we touch a child. A child calling 911 can have you in jail, just for correcting him or her. A teacher cannot touch a child because that breeds violence.

Listen to what Rosemond also says.

> As the occasional warning, I spank my children. I did so not because I had given it a lot of thought or believe the children need to be spanked or had reached the end of my rope, but simply because I felt like it.
>
> I have learned this with the 20 years of raising my children, to trust my feelings. You see, to spank or not to spank is not the question. The question in regards to what you do and don't do is simply this; does it work? (*He discovered it worked. So he used it.*)
>
> Twelve years ago, I wrote a newspaper column that stated spanking was not the big bad thing it was made out to be. As that column appeared, one such made for a big deal. She told me I had, in effect, endorsed child abuse.
>
> Another person on my editors' staff was disturbed because it played right into the hands of people with a "spare the rod, spoil the child" mentality.*
>
> What really disturbed my critics is that I don't share their view of the world, part of which include a myth that says children who are spanked hate themselves for being such rotten kids, learn to solve problems by hitting people, will someday abuse their own children, become violent criminals or all of the above.
>
> I have good news. Those lists are wrong. The social, economic, political, psychological facts

---

* This is a reference to believers who embrace and practice what Proverbs 13:24 says, "He that spareth his rod hateth his son: but he that loveth him chasteneth him betimes."

combined to produce criminals, child abusers, bullies and emotional cripples are far too complex for even a computer to fathom. To suggest a spanking plays a major role in shaping that child's social behavior is ludicrous. It is lack of belief to even think that spanking is a cause of our violence, in the school today or our criminals. In fact, it's just the reverse. If there had been more spankings, there would be fewer kids out of control today. There would be kids with more respect for authority. There would be kids better behaved in society and know how to live in society, if parents would have gone back to the Word of God to raise their children."[11] (*Italicized* words in parenthesis added by Dr. Allen)

Reggie White has written a tremendous book, Fighting The Good Fight.[12] He has a section called, "Whooping." He expresses why I believe in whooping too. He says, "I believe that spanking, or whooping, as I called them, are important for raising kids the right way."[13] He also says, "I can assure you that I am no worse for the wear, if fact. I know I am a better person because my mother cared enough to do that to me."[14]

You see, it is hard to discipline children. It takes time and attention. More importantly, it is hard to inflict pain on kids, which is necessary to teach them a lesson. I think it's one of the hardest things we do as parents. To tell you the truth, the last two times I whooped my kids, I cried, but I knew I had done the right thing by them. When I whoop them, I just don't walk away afterwards. After they calm down, I have them explain to me why I whipped them. When they "'fess up" to what they have done, and it comes from their mouth, they'll remember why they were punished.

Every child understands pain. That's how we learn. Children may look like angels, but we all know they aren't. If left to their own devices, they will turn into little terrorists. I believe we are born with original sin. We have a naturally selfish nature. The only way to teach

---

[11] ibid.
[12] Fighting The Good Fight, Reggie White, Thomas Nelson Inc (June 1999), ISBN: 978-0785269649
[13] ibid.
[14] ibid.

children to not be that way is for parents to constantly be on them, watching, correcting and once in a while spanking or whooping them to get their obedience. Fighting The Good Fight is a tremendous book, and the author has many other comments about whipping and spanking.

Spank or not to spank is not the question. Our church has a staff that believes in spanking. All of our staff, the pastoral staff, grew up in homes where spanking was the rule of the day. It was something that was done on a regular basis. We talked about Jim, who had that rod in the home, had that strap on the wall with a sign over it that says, "I need thee every hour." **As children, some of us "need it every hour." And, some of us got it on a regular basis. So, in this church you have staff that endorses spanking. So don't come to any of us and try to get a contrary view, which you will not get.

I thought today, I've talked about Jim, and I've talked about Kenneth, so Terry, would you come tell us the last time you got a spanking?*** Terry, can you remember that far back, or did it make that much of an impression on you? Tell us about your spanking experience.

Terry said,

> "I never was a mean boy like Jim and Kenneth!" (*the congregation roared with laughter at this point*). But, I did get one spanking that I remember and I think it was the last one.
>
> I was raised on a farm in southeast Alabama. We raised and grew crops, cotton, corn and peanuts. How many of you... the younger generation won't identify with this at all. How many of you have ever picked cotton in your life? If you look around, those who have are probably older than they are younger, but I picked cotton.
>
> My father was not an educated man, so far as book learning was going. My father was in 4th, 5th and 6th grades in different subject areas. He went to a one-room school house, like you might have read about.

** Here Dr. Allen refers to Jim Garner, who he spoke about in Chapter 7, page 77.
*** Terry Killingsworth was the Music Minister at Peachtree City Baptist Church at the time of this sermon. Kenneth Brown was the Assistant Minister at that time.

But he was a smart man; he knew what not to do and when not to do it.

We picked cotton and put some in a trailer, which was actually a wagon with higher boards to make it hold more. My father told me one day, 'Get up there and help pack that cotton down with your feet, so that the trailer will hold more.'

Now, in picking cotton, the burrs sometimes come loose from the cotton stalk, through weathering, and they have sharp points on them. I made the mistake, after he told me to get up there and pack that cotton, of starting my sentence with, 'I ain't gonna do it.' But, I didn't get it out of my mouth because I had no shoes on. Cotton stocks grew very high and were woody kinds of plants, and he jerked one out of the ground. And when he finished there was about 8-10 inches left in his hand. The rest of it was scattered around on the ground. But you know what; I packed that cotton with no shoes on."

Thank you, Terry. I tell you what, you never know what you are going to get from Terry when you call on him, but that's great. He remembers though, and he's a survivor!

AUTHORITY, RESPECT, LOVE AND SPANKING

Let me ask, "Why do you spank? Why is it necessary? Why do you have to spank?" I think, first of all, you spank just to remind the child who's in charge. To remind him or her that you are the authority, and that you are teaching respect for authority. The child's word is not the last word. Whatever the issue is, it is not up for negotiation, it is not up for debate, and it's not up for a vote. You must remind the child that you are in charge, that you are the head of the home.

We must teach the children these things. Sometimes we must reinforce it, by spanking. I think you must spank because you love your child. You can't say, "I love my child too much to hit my child." No, that's not true. If you love your child, you will inflict pain on your child when correction warrants it. If you love your child, you will spank when a child does wrong, because you are teaching the child some valuable lessons. You do it out of love, not because you just want to hit your child.

> ***Proverbs 13:24*** He that spareth his rod hateth his son:
> but he that loveth him chasteneth him betimes.

This is the Word of God. It's not the preacher saying it. It's not John Rosemond, or a psychiatrist, or a psychologist saying it... it is God. He who spares the rod hates his son, but he who loves his son is careful to discipline him. If you love your child, you are going to care enough to bring discipline.

> ***Proverbs 29:15*** The rod and reproof give wisdom: but
> a child left *to himself* bringeth his mother to shame.

A child left to himself disgraces his mother. Children are born with original sin. Children are born with a bent towards evil. Children are born with a dark side. That precious little baby has it in him the potential to become a "public enemy number one!" It's that sin nature that must be corrected, must be told, must be disciplined, and must be changed.

Yesterday on Fox News, I listened to the news about the shooting and the crime, and all the experts are all trying to find a way to blame somebody else.**** They certainly are not going to blame themselves for the poor advice they have been giving us for 30 years. They had a district attorney from Milwaukee on the news show, and he blurted out to one of them, "Don't tell me that! Children are born savages and they must be trained! I know because I've got three!"

That's true; they are! Children are born savages. Babies are savages, if left to themselves. They must be trained and disciplined. If left to themselves, they will disgrace their mother.

> ***Proverbs 22:15*** Foolishness *is* bound in the heart of a
> child; *but* the rod of correction shall drive it far from
> him.

**** Dr. Allen is referring to the Columbine Massacre that happened a couple weeks prior to this sermon, in April 20, 1999. The killings took place in Littleton, Colorado.

That precious little baby has it in him, a lot of violence, a lot of tendency to do wrong, and it is bound up in the heart. And, the Bible says that "the rod of discipline will drive it far from him."

Notice that the rod of discipline will drive it from him. You love the child, and you teach the child self-discipline by spanking. This does not mean child abuse. Don't misunderstand me. I abhor child abuse. I think people who abuse a child ought to be put *under* the jail for life!

There is a way to spank in love, in tenderness and still let the child know you are the authority. You teach the child that you are the authority. You teach the child respect and you are helping the child learn self-control.

COMMUNICATION AND SPANKING

There is a lot of talk about gun control these days, and I don't like guns. I don't have a gun in my house. I don't believe in guns, and they aren't the problem we face. The problem that we face is training children.

I was reminded of a mother that told the neighbors she was having trouble with her little boy, Johnny.

She said, "I don't understand little Johnny. I fenced in the back yard and he learned how to lift the latch and get out. So, I raised the latch. Then he got a little stool, got up on it and lifted the latch and got out."

She continued, "I raised the latch higher and he got a stool and a stick. With the stick, he lifted the latch."

And the wise neighbor said, "I suggest you put the latch on Johnny, not on the gate."

I think that's where "the latch" needs to be. Put the latch on Johnny. And let him know what behavior is not acceptable, and start young. Let children know what behavior isn't wanted.

So, when do you spank? You spank when a child is willfully disobedient. You don't spank them because of irresponsibility. All children are irresponsible, just like some of us adults are irresponsible. You don't spank them because they spilled their milk, because they knocked over a vase, because they forgot to feed the dog, because they left their bicycle out, lost their bicycle, or because they left their jacket at school or at church. You don't spank them because of that, that's children being children. That's just irresponsibility from being a child!

You spank them when they challenge you; that is when they are asking for it! When they challenge your authority, that's when they are being willfully disobedient. When you tell your child to do something or not do something, and he or she totally disregards your word, that's when you must teach them.

When our little granddaughter, Tori, was 3 years old, we were riding in the car one day. She got in the car with a little bowl of dry cereal. I looked over and saw her playing with the cereal and I said, "Tori, don't spill the cereal in the car."

We drove a little while and she looked up at me. I saw her out of the corner of my eye when she took that bowl of cereal and just turned it upside down, pouring it all over the car! Well, I stopped the car and spanked her. It shocked her, but she never spilt any more cereal in the car. She was being willfully disobedient. She was three years old, and yet she was testing me. She was challenging my authority. I cried, and of course she cried, but everything was fine. She had to know that I could not allow that to happen. I had a responsibility: she was under my care.*****

A few months later, my son called one night and asked, "Daddy, did you spank Tori?"

I asked, "Well, what did she say?"

He said, "Well, we were driving down the road and everything was quiet. All of the sudden Tori spoke and said, 'Grandpa spanked me.' It was out of the blue! I said, 'He did?' And Tori said, 'Yeah, he spanked me.' I asked Tori, 'Well, why did he spank you?' And she said, 'Because he told me not to pour the cereal out and I did anyway!'"

You see, she knew! She understood. We are still close today. But, Tori understood that was a test. She had just come home from Africa with my son. They were serving in the mission field, and she was deciding what the boundaries were with granddad.

Children do that and you have to decide who's going to be in charge. Who's going to run the house? Who's going to make the decisions? You have to make that decision for the children by sometimes inflicting a little pain to let them know the answer!

You have to define the boundaries ahead of time. You don't spank because they do something that crosses a boundary you haven't explained ahead of time. I told Tori not to do something in advance.

***** Later in her young life, Tori Allen would be the youngest woman ever to climb El Capitan in Yosemite National Park (September 10, 2001) – age 13. She also won the gold medal for speed climbing in the 2002 X-Games – age 14.

She did it anyway. She knew the boundaries, so it was appropriate she suffer the consequences.

You have to define the boundaries before you enforce them. Let your children know what to expect.

Don't hit your children and run. Stay around to love them, dry their tears if necessary, and have them explain back to you why they were punished. They have to respond and let you know that they understood. That's why you don't spank them a long time after they cross a boundary. You spank immediately. You don't put it off.

Saying, "I'm gonna spank you when I get home," or "Daddy is going to spank you when he gets home," loses the proper effect of the spanking. You do it immediately in response to when the child crosses the boundary. This is when they know what they have done and they have a chance to let you know what they have done.

I know its difficult today. If you spank a child today in public, you could be in trouble. Today I heard about a 7th grader in Washington D.C. The mother had gone to pick him up early from school. The child had left home that morning dressed in some nice khaki pants and shirt. When the mother got to school, the boy had changed clothes. He had put on a tank top and baggy pants, and she found him that way when she picked him up. She was upset, and rightly so. She went to the principal and asked if there was a vacant room some place. She took her boy into a special room, a spanking room, and she turned him over and gave him a good spanking in that room.

He was in 7th grade. That macho child got a spanking. When it was over, he came out and reported it the principal. The principal responded, "I'm not going to do anything; your mother may come over here and spank me!"

We need more principals like that. Let the mother do what she felt she needed to do when she caught the boy, who was being disobedient and disrespectful to her wishes. He was showing disrespect, because she sent him to school one way and he chose to dress another way after he got to school. That's disrespecting her authority. That's disrespecting who she is, and when children disrespect authority, they need to be punished. They need to be reminded. If they don't respect their parents, how are they going to respect a policeman, a teacher, or anyone else in authority?

The reason we have so much chaos in the school today is because children are not taught to respect their parents. They go to school and they don't respect anybody. If your child is like this, then chances are that someday you will visit him in a penitentiary. He won't respect the guards there, but he will have to do what they say. There have to be some guidelines, some boundaries.

Don't wait until it's too late.

> ***Proverbs 19:18*** Chasten thy son while there is hope, and let not thy soul spare for his crying.

Discipline and chasten your children while there is hope, while they are young. I don't recommend that you spank a child while he is one year old or a few months old, because they don't really understand. At that age they are great imitators. If you pick up something to look at it, or a friend does, then really young children are going to pick up the same thing to look at. What you need to do, when they are very young, is just take the temptation away from them. If you have a vase you don't want them to touch, then you move it. You put it up high. You take things off the table that they might be tempted to play with, because they don't understand; they are just great imitators.

But when children get to be about 2 years of age, this is a time when you start the process of spanking. If you have a very smart child, you might start a little younger. Regardless, you let them know about boundaries. Start with just giving them a little sting, not child abuse. I am not talking about child abuse here, I am not telling you to spank out of anger or frustration either. Instead, use spanking as a method of teaching and training and directing your child.

Ages 2 to 6 are the crucial years. Those are the molding years. If you don't get your child under control by the time he is 6, you are going to lose the battle. If they talk back to you, show disrespect for your word or your command, and you think that is cute so you laugh rather than correct them, then they will go through life thinking the whole world will laugh when they do something. One day they are going to grow up and it's not going to be so cute anymore.

Kids often talk back, thinking the idea that they have a right, but no, no, no, no! They don't have the right to talk back! They may have some privileges, but you have a responsibility to be in authority, and that responsibility isn't over for years. You must teach your children how to live in society. You must teach and train them, so that they can be civilized in a civilized world. This is your responsibility, and those early years are important.

In our church, we have a family that has a boy that is seven years of age. When he was getting ready for his seventh birthday, he was so excited about his upcoming birthday. He was going to have a party, and all of his friends were coming to visit.

This boy came home from school one day with a yellow card. The yellow card means he misbehaved in school. The mother sat down and talked to her boy. She said, "Now, you've got this yellow card. If you get another yellow card before your birthday, we will not have a birthday party."

A couple of days before his birthday party, the boy came in with another yellow card. Now his mother was really in quandary. She had said what was going to happen. She had put down a boundary. So, she called off the party, but she didn't call the kids to tell them this news. The mother made her boy pick up the phone and call every child who was invited. The mother let her boy tell the children that there was not going to be a birthday party.

One of the little fella's friends asked him, "Why are we not having the party?"

The boy replied, "Because I was disobedient in school."

You see, that mother's boy got the message. He'll always remember the non-birthday party that he had when he was seven years old. They didn't have it.

The mother she cried all afternoon, but she did what she said she was going to do. She backed up her words. She taught a lesson that cost her much, and she paid the price and suffered the hurt. The boy was hurt too, but she knew that she was right and it was her responsibility. She was not his mom just so she could make him happy. She was the mother who must prepare her boy for the future. She was there to make a boy into a man. Sometimes it hurts; it hurts the parents. You take the responsibility; it hurts, but you do it.

There are many ways you might discipline at home. You might tell a teenager, who is 30 minutes late coming home, that he can't have the car for a week, or he can't watch TV for two nights. You put some restrictions in place.

Eventually the children go off to college. At that point, it is kind of difficult to spank them; although, I spanked mine. In college, my youngest son got into some trouble. He had been drinking. I was trying to communicate with him, and he kind of sassed me. I took off my belt. We tore up grass in the backyard! We plowed up the yard as I chased my son through the backyard. I thought I'd probably be in jail if anybody saw me.

I was wrong to do that, but I had to reinforce what I taught him earlier. He had forgotten, and I had the responsibility to remind him who was in charge. I did have other alternatives. I could have cut off the money, the finances he relied on from me in college. I considered that. I could have said, "No, I'm not going to finance him at college!" But, I had to get his attention before I could talk to him. It is important that you get their attention, so you can teach them.

We laugh about that whole story today. Perhaps you know that my youngest son is a preacher today! He went to Africa as a missionary. Evidently the spanking did not cause him to be a violent criminal, but he did know that his dad was in charge. My view was, "As long as you get your meals from me, as long as you put your feet under my table, then dad is in charge."

That's the way I was raised. When you can pay your own way, when you buy your own car, when you buy your own gas, when you buy your own clothes, when you pay your own tuition at college, then at that point you can do whatever you want to do. As long as I am paying for most of those things, I am in charge. It's not harsh. That's the way it ought to be, and that's what the Bible says... you have to have control, in order to establish what is right.

I think that during a spanking, using your hand is probably the best way you ought to do it. That way you know you won't hit too hard because it will hurt you about as much as it hurt the child. It will sting you too. So use your hands, and never hit your child in the face. Never hit them there. God prepared the best place. It is a perfect place. It is just right, because it is padded and it bends well. You just bend that child over, and the right spanking spot is on his back end! God knew what He was doing when He made a place for paddling. For that spot, using your hand will be fine.

Again, don't hit your children with your fist, and don't hit them in the face. Hit them with your hand outstretched like this across their behind and they'll get the message. That would be good.

LIFE AND SPANKING

What is the purpose of spanking? I think ultimately the main reason for spanking and discipline is you are preparing your child for life's decisions. Life's ultimate decision is to accept Jesus Christ as Savior, and to be committed to Him.

You have the responsibility as a parent to prepare your children, so that they will come to know God. This what the writer of Hebrews is saying,

> ***Hebrews 12:9-10*** Furthermore we have had fathers of our flesh which corrected *us*, and we gave *them* reverence: shall we not much rather be in subjection unto the Father of spirits, and live? For they verily for a few days chastened *us* after their own pleasure; but he for *our* profit, that *we* might be partakers of his holiness.

Your earthly father punished, disciplined, and chastened you. Your earthly father did this for your own good. God does the same thing. You understand that you are to learn right and wrong from your earthly father. He confronts you with the guilt of what you have done. He teaches you what is right. A parent, who loves their children, confronts them when they do wrong. There are consequences. So, parents have the responsibility to confront the children out of love, in order to correct what is wrong.

As a child gets older, he begins to think, "Wait just a minute, my heavenly Father has spelled out some things that I am not to do. My heavenly Father confronts me with my sins too. So, there is going to be punishment if I don't do something about my behavior."

Thus, it leads our children to repent.

> ***Proverbs 23:13*** Withhold not correction from the child: for *if* thou beatest him with the rod, he shall not die. Thou shalt beat him with the rod, and shalt deliver his soul from hell.

You're not dying when you use a rod, but if you don't use "the rod" you may die spiritually because you haven't taught what's right and what's wrong. You do not teach with a sense of guilt, but with a desire to encourage the salvation experience, understand that.

Discipline produces a harvest of righteousness and peace for those who have been trained by it. Those who train, by discipline, have a harvest of righteousness. We respect God as we respect our earthly father. You see, if that child doesn't respect his earthly parents, then he will think he can do whatever he pleases. He will think he can give in to his own selfish desires and his own selfish urges, just living life the way he wants to. He thinks that if he is in control, then he doesn't need God. He says, "I am not going to respect God the Father." But if he learns to respect his earthly authority in his earthly father, then that teaches him to respect his heavenly Father. It teaches the child that God loves him.

Thank You, Father, for today and the blessings of it. Father, help us be good parents and grandparents. Help us to draw the line, to be the example and to teach our children to respect those above them, those in authority, so when they grow up they will respect You, honor You and serve You, Lord. In Christ's name, Amen.

The Allens: David, Nancy, Harold, Stephen
(from left to right)

CHAPTER 9: BLESSING YOUR CHILD

First Baptist Church, Peachtree City, Georgia
May 30, 1999

The elderly Isaac was ready to give his blessing to his eldest son.

It was a custom in Biblical times for the father to pass down a blessing to his children. What is a blessing? It is an acceptance. The blessing is to give the child prestige, authority and inheritance. The elder son got more than the other children, thus the elder son received the first blessing. The father would give him that special blessing. It recognized him as the leader of the family, and distributed to him his share of inheritance.

This was a Biblical custom, and it's a great custom. It is a custom that we need to give to our children, a blessing. We don't need to wait until they are 40 years old or when we are about to die. We should give it from the time they are born. We need to give them approval, acceptance, love, and encouragement. That is what the blessing is.

Some children spend their whole life seeking acceptance from their parents... really seeking a blessing from their parents. How they receive acceptance, a blessing from their parents, will affect how they feel about themselves, and what they pass on to their children. So it is so important that we, as parents, give our children that blessing.

When Isaac called for Esau, he said it was time for the blessing. Isaac said, "Go out into the field and kill game and bring it to me. Fix some stew, and after we have had our meal together, I will give you the blessing."

Jacob was the younger of the two brothers, though they were twins. Jacob was a few minutes younger than Esau. That made him the second born, and he was a deceiver, a schemer. The boys were twins, yet totally different. Esau was an outdoorsman. Jacob was a domestic person; he stayed at home and was closer to his mother.

The mother played favorites at the time of Isaac's blessing. She said to the younger son, Jacob, "Hurry, let's fix some venison while

101

your brother is gone. You can take it to your dad, and you can receive the blessing… the blessing for the elder son!"

And that's what happened. Because Jacob was physically different from Esau, Jacob put on the clothes of the older brother. So, he smelled like an outdoorsman, like one who had been out in the field. Jacob's hands were smooth, so he and his mother took the skin of a lamb that they had killed and tied it on Jacob's arms. Isaac was an elderly man and was almost blind. When Isaac felt Jacob's hand, it felt rough, like that of Esau.

I do not want to address the deceiving part of this story, which is for another sermon. Let's look at the blessing part, when Isaac gave the blessing.

> ***Genesis 27:22-29*** And Jacob went near unto Isaac his father; and he felt him, and said, The voice *is* Jacob's voice, but the hands *are* the hands of Esau. And he discerned him not, because his hands were hairy, as his brother Esau's hands: so he blessed him. And he said, *Art* thou my very son Esau? And he said, I *am*. And he said, Bring *it* near to me, and I will eat of my son's venison, that my soul may bless thee. And he brought *it* near to him, and he did eat: and he brought him wine, and he drank. And his father Isaac said unto him, Come near now, and kiss me, my son. And he came near, and kissed him: and he smelled the smell of his raiment, and blessed him, and said, See, the smell of my son *is* as the smell of a field which the LORD hath blessed: Therefore God give thee of the dew of heaven, and the fatness of the earth, and plenty of corn and wine: Let people serve thee, and nations bow down to thee: be lord over thy brethren, and let thy mother's sons bow down to thee: cursed *be* every one that curseth thee, and blessed *be* he that blesseth thee.

Last week we talked about spanking,[*] and we talked about correcting a child. This week I want to talk about praising a child. This is the other side of the coin. It is the other side of the record, so to speak.

---

[*] This message is Chapter 8: To Spank or Not To Spank.

There is a time for discipline, a time when there is some spanking, but there must be even more time of loving, acceptance, and praising the child. Let your children know they have worth. These are ways that we can give the gift of blessing.

BLESSING THROUGH MEANINGFUL TOUCH

Notice that Isaac said to his son, "Come near to me. Let me touch you. Come and kiss me." Jacob is 40 years old, but he's given a touch, and his father is giving a touch to him.

A meaningful touch means so much to children. So I say to you, parents learn how to show affection, if you don't already know. Reach out. Maybe you had parents who never touched you much, never hugged you much, and never gave you assurance. Well, you break that cycle right now. When you start, give your child some hugs and some loving, some tender caress. Will you do it all their lives, when they are little and when they get older? I still hug my boys when I see them. I kiss them because I am glad to see them, and they hug me back. We touch. Touch conveys so much. It conveys you are loved and you are appreciated.

> ***Mark 10:14*** But when Jesus saw *it*, he was much displeased, and said unto them, Suffer the little children to come unto me, and forbid them not: for of such is the kingdom of God.

Jesus had the little children to come to him. He didn't just speak to the little children at a distance. He sat down, He sat the children on his lap, and He hugged them, He touched them. Jesus conveyed to them that He cared about them.

Remember on another occasion what He did to the leper, the guy that had leprosy all over his body (Matthew 8:1-3). It was interesting that as the man with leprosy came to see Jesus, Jesus did not heal him *and then* touch him. Jesus touched him, and then healed him. Jesus was saying, "I care about you." And, Jesus was willing to touch the man whose body was covered in leprosy because his spiritual need was greater than his physical need. The leper had the need of acceptance and to be a part of someone or something.

I know we live in a day and age when people have been concerned about inappropriate touching. I abhor inappropriate touching and certainly feel that we need to condemn it in every way. I think that because of inappropriate touching we have lost some of the innocence of children. I believe parents could hug their children and kiss them as they grow up. Praise them, put your hand on their shoulder, play with them, and rub on their hair, even though they get upset at you. Rub on their hair a little bit and let them know you care about them. They may fuss, but they will remember the fact that you acknowledged their presence and gave them worth. A meaningful touch is so important; it is a way to give a blessing to your children. Hold them, watch them, and read to them. These are ways of saying, "I care about you."

BLESSING THROUGH THE SPOKEN WORD

Beyond meaningful touch, there is the spoken word. It is not enough just to hug without saying anything. You need to speak words of praise to your children.

The word *bless* means "to enrich." You enrich someone by giving them praise. You don't enrich them by criticizing them, tearing them down and making fun of them. You don't enrich them by fussing at them all the time saying, "You are so clumsy, you're so stupid, you won't ever amount to anything," or "You are so lazy." Those things do not enhance or enrich a child.

"You are doing a great job!" "Oh, the yard looks so good!" "Your room looks wonderful!" "You've done a good job, I'm so proud of you!" "You got a good grade!" These are ways of speaking words of encouragement.

When your girl washes the dishes, you say, "Oh they look so good, I am so proud of you." She goes to bed, and you wash the dishes again and put them away, but you don't do it in front of her.

You know that when your boy cuts the grass, you don't get in a fuss because he didn't put the lawnmower away, or because there is a little bit of grass on the sidewalk! You praise him for what he has done. Praise is so important to children. You can never give a child too much praise. Let them know you care and that you are proud of them.

Let me say this; don't praise children just when they do something spectacular. Sometimes you might make that mistake. Don't just praise them when they get the good grades, achieve the awards, or when they do something particularly important. Otherwise, they will get the idea that the only time that they are going to be accepted is when they do something outstanding. They might spend their whole lives struggling, trying to succeed, and trying to be first in the class, trying to make good grades because they think, "I will not be accepted unless I do something out of the ordinary." No, you give it to them when they do the little things. You praise them for who they are, and not for what they do or for what they achieve. You praise them for who they are, not for what they do or what they say. You give them praise.

Isaac said to Jacob, "Oh wonderful, you smell like a field!" I am not sure that that is a compliment for us today, to smell like someone who has been out in a barnyard, but for Isaac, it was a compliment. We might find something else to put in place of that and say something like, "You're the best thing that's ever happened to me! I'm so proud of you. You are the best Christmas present I ever had!" Communicate to your children that they have worth and value, and that they are not a burden or trouble. We don't regret to have them. They have great value; you must communicate that to them.

So, how do you do that? You do it by talking to them, on their level, eye to eye. You do it by listening to them when you talk. I know you can't do it all day long, but listen to your children when they have something to say.

Let's say you're reading the paper and they come in and want to talk. You lay the newspaper aside and talk. If they come in during the middle of the ball game and it's tied up, first of the ninth, but they want to talk, then turn off the TV. You communicate to them by doing this: showing that they are more important than a ball game. Show them that they are more important than the newspaper, that they are more important than the work you brought home to do, which you should have done at the office but because you goofed off all day and took coffee breaks, you had to bring home to make up for the time you lost at work. Don't take the time away from your children and rob them of the time they deserve. Communicate that they have worth. Communicate that they are worth your time. Don't take off with the fellas, but rather take your children to McDonald's, to play Putt-Putt Golf, or take them on vacation.

Having said that, I think the marriage is primary. I think a lot of folks make mistakes with this one. The relationship between husband and wife is more important than any other in the home. That relationship must be maintained above the mother's relationship with children. Don't lose sight of that. Husbands and wives need weekends together, vacations together, and they need time away from their children to renew their marriage and keep it alive and fresh. That is important.

At the same time, your children need you to give them some time. They need to go with you on vacation sometimes. They need to go with you to Disney World. Wherever you go, they need some time. Spend time with your children. In doing that you are communicating they have worth and they have value. Isaac communicated to his son that he had worth. Let your children know that they have great worth. Give them your time. And then, as you give them your blessing, picture a positive future for them. That's important.

Write or draw a picture of something positive for your children. Isaac said to Jacob, "Someday nations are going to bow down to you. Some day you are going to have a place of authority and prestige." Well, the next 20 years were going to be rugged for old Jacob. He didn't have anything. He was struggling, but he had that picture of the future, that someday he would have something. His father gave him the picture of a great future.

Picture a positive future for your child. "You'll never learn," or "You are too dumb to learn," or "You'll never do this," or "You'll never do that," or "You are too lazy," or "Nobody will ever marry you," or "You'll never please anybody," these words are negative.

BLESSING THROUGH A SENSITIVE HEART

You have to have a sensitive heart to paint a positive picture for your children. Some days you might say they'll be a nurse, or whatever is their passion. Some days you might say they'll be a doctor. You might say, "Oh, you are such a quick learner, you would make a great teacher!" You might say, "You love animals; I can just see it now! Someday, you will be taking care of animals." You might say, "You love people. God has something special for you."

Can you picture these positive pictures?

> ***Proverbs 22:6*** Train up a child in the way he should
> go: and when he is old, he will not depart from it.

Raise a child, not the way *you think* he should go, but the way the Bible says he should go. A child comes to you being "bent" in certain ways God sees fit. So, you study the child, you learn the abilities of the child and you help guide the child in the way he or she is "bent" – not in the way you would like them to be "bent!"

In the movie, *Dead Poet Society*, there was a story about a young man. His father was a doctor. He had great plans for his son. His son went to prep school, and he wanted to be an actor in the movies. He was selected for one of the plays on campus, and he got his father to come. Even though his father was very reluctant to come, he did come the night of the play. The boy did an outstanding job. He did a great job in acting, and he received a standing ovation when it was over.

After the play, the father walked to the son and said, "Son, I am not going to let you ruin your life! You are not going to throw your life way, and I am taking you out of this school. I am putting you in the Military Academy because I am not going to let you waste your life with dreams."

That night the boy killed himself. It was so sad, because he didn't fit into his father's dreams. God had given him a different dream. The boy was marching to the tune of a different drum, and the father couldn't accept it.

If your children are bent on doing something specific in life, then encourage them that way. Paint a positive picture of their future.

Sandra was born in the barren part of Arizona, about 200 miles from El Paso, where her mother delivered her. She grew up in an adobe house. She had no electricity, she had no water, she was from a poor area, and there was no school. Her mother had to teach her at home. The mother subscribed to magazines, and these were the reading materials for Sandra.

Every summer, Sandra's mother and father would get in the old station wagon, load up the kids, and visit different state capitals. They visited every capital west of the Mississippi. They would go to the capital, they would walk up the steps, they would go to the dome, and talk about the state capital they were visiting. Every summer, that is the way they spent their vacation.

The whole time, the mother and father were painting positive pictures for their children from the adobe house on that large ranch in Mexico. When the little girl did grow up, the parents had done a good job. She got into college: Stanford University. From there she went to law school, and not long ago she was selected to be the first female Chief Justice of the United States, Sandra Day O'Conner.

Sandra made it because she was intellectual and she worked hard. But, I think she made it also because she had a mother and father that painted a positive picture for her. They didn't tell her she would never amount to anything, or that she was limited. They kept good things before her all the time, painting a picture. She could do anything she wanted to do with her life.

One extreme is Marsha. Marsha was a slow learner, who couldn't do very much. An assignment that took other kids 30 minutes might take her an hour and a half or two hours to do. Marsha's mother didn't say, "Hurry up, hurry up and get it done! Don't be so slow!" Her mother said, "I am so proud of you! You stay right with it! You finish your assignment, even if it takes you longer! I am proud of you as you struggle to do it." Marsha's mother noticed that Marsha had a way of communicating with her younger sisters, and also with the neighbor's children. So her mother said, "Why don't you come to Sunday school and you can help me and dad, as we work with the children?"

So, Marsha started going to Sunday school with mom and dad. She would help with those children in their early years of education. Then one day, she came home and she said, "When I grow up, I am going to be a teacher." Marsha's parents didn't laugh. They didn't make fun of Marsha. They didn't say, "Now Marsha, don't think too high because you know you can't do it! We think it is wonderful, but there is no way."

Marsha was struggling and was at the bottom of her class. But, her parents knew that she was going to be a teacher someday. They said, "Well, honey, if that is what you want to do, we will do what we can to help you and support you."

In her elementary school years, Marsha's parents hired tutors. In high school, they hired tutors to come read to her to help her along. She made it through high school and went on to college. On her commencement day, she walked across the platform to receive her diploma!

Marsha had what a lot of folks had in that day. She already had a job. As a student teacher that year, she taught first grade at school. She did such a great job. She communicated to the kids so well. She had so much love and sympathy for the kids that the principal recognized her and gave her a job as soon as she received her degree.

Who said she couldn't do it? Her mother didn't and her daddy didn't, though society might have. She was still a slow learner, but she reached her capacity because they painted a bright picture for her.

Your child, whether a slow learner or not, needs to have that positive future always out there, painted for them, about what they can do with their lives and how it can amount to something. Paint a good picture for your child.

BLESSING THROUGH COMMITMENT

The mortar that holds meaningful touch, the spoken word, and the sensitive heart together is commitment. You have to make a commitment. There is a cost to raising children. I don't mean financial cost, but something more than that. It does cost time, effort, and resources, but it also costs a lot of prayer. It costs commitment.

When you have children, you make a commitment to them and you must pay that price. You must pay the commitment of prayer. Pray for your children, and pray that God will guide them.

The other night Catherine Bell got married here. She is Susan Bell's daughter, and it was a beautiful wedding, Cathy grew up here, a sweet little girl. She stood up here and they took a picture. Tommy was standing beside her; he's a wonderful young man. Then someone made a comment about a beautiful couple, and the mother of Thomas said, "Oh, she's the answer to my prayer. The day Thomas was born I began to pray for the girl that he would marry."

She had spent those years praying for the mate for her son. I must confess I didn't do that with my boys, but wish I had. It's not too late for some of you. We can do it with our grandchildren. Begin to pray that God will bring the right person into their lives, that God will protect them. That's costly, to spend time in prayer for your children.

If your kid has a thing for the piano, then you give them lessons. You might think, "I can't afford it!" Oh yes, you can. You buy an old piano if you have to. Get them the lessons. You use your resources to develop that child. This is a commitment on your part: to help your child.

I was talking to a young couple last night; well, they aren't that young. I want you to know that 30 is really young, 40 is really young. You may think you older folks can't teach them anything, but that's a young age for teaching. Anyway, this couple has a daughter. She's a beautiful, wonderful, and precious Christian girl going off to college. In the conversation, we talked about why she chose the college she chose. It is out of state, more expensive, and it is a real financial sacrifice for the couple to pay what it's going to take for her to go to college there.

Their daughter looked around at some schools. As a fine Christian girl, she came to the conclusion that she wanted to go to a Christian college. It would help her enrich her faith and challenge her faith, not destroy her faith. She wanted to go someplace, to a school where her faith would be strengthened and not weakened. She shared that with her mom and dad. She told them, "I'd like to go to this college because I know that this college will strengthen my faith."

And her daddy, with tears in his eyes, said, "Alright, you can go there. We will do what we have to do to make it positive."

Now, he may have to get another job, although I don't know how he could because he already works all the time. He will do what he has to, that is what he was simply saying.

He was saying, "Whatever resources I have, I will make it available for you to have the environment and the education you need." That's commitment. You make those commitments with your children, and when you do, you don't look back.

Well we've talked about the gift of blessing. There is a lot more I could say, but you might want to read the book, The Gift of the Blessing.[15] It's about children who don't get the blessing, children that get the blessing, and how you get the blessing to your children. Give the blessing to your children. Give them meaningful touches as they grow up. Speak words of praise and encouragement to them. Communicate their worth. Picture a positive future for them, and make the commitment it takes to bring it all together.

Susanne Wesley raised 19 children. They all turned out pretty good. John Wesley was a preacher who led great revivals. Charles Wesley wrote many of the songs that we sing. The other children were all very productive in life.

Someone asked Susanne Wesley, "How did you produce so many wonderful children?" She said, "It was quite simple. In the kitchen I had a switch and an apple. When they were bad I used the switch, when they were good I gave them the apple."

She was simply saying there are times of discipline and there are times for praise. Don't get that out of balance. Remember that you can't give too much praise. Some people say praise is like perfume; it smells good, but too much stinks! Well, that doesn't work with children when it comes to praise. I have never known a child that left home and said, "My parents gave me too much acceptance, too much approval, too much praise, too much love or too much encouragement." I have never had a child in all my life say that their parents gave them too much love or acceptance or approval. Give them that love.

---

[15] The Gift of the Blessing, Dr. John Trent and Dr. Gary Smalley, Thomas Nelson Publishers; Revised edition (July 14, 1993), ISBN 978-0840748492

When you think about it, God is the ultimate Father. Our model Father touched us, and as He became flesh and bone among us He took on our form to be one of us. In this way He touched us. He spoke to us. Jesus says, "...he that loveth me shall be loved of my Father, and I will love him..." (John 14:21).

Our Father pictured a wonderful future for us. Jesus said, "In my Father's house are many mansions: if *it were* not *so*, I would have told you. I go to prepare a place for you" (John 14:2).

Jesus gave us a sense of self-worth in that He paid the price for us. And, He made the commitment, the ultimate commitment. He died on the cross, so that you and I might have eternal life. Make the commitment to give your children the gift of blessing, and to teach them to seek the blessing of a relationship with Jesus.

Dr. Allen with his sons, David (center) and Stephen (right)

Dr. David Allen (left) in his Doctorate Robe with his father,
Dr. Harold Allen at his side (right)

CHAPTER 10: RELEASING YOUR CHILD

First Baptist Church, Peachtree City, Georgia
<u>June 6, 1999</u>

1 Samuel 1:21-28 And the man Elkanah, and all his house, went up to offer unto the LORD the yearly sacrifice, and his vow. But Hannah went not up; for she said unto her husband, *I will not go up* until the child be weaned, and *then* I will bring him, that he may appear before the LORD, and there abide for ever. And Elkanah her husband said unto her, Do what seemeth thee good; tarry until thou have weaned him; only the LORD establish his word. So the woman abode, and gave her son suck until she weaned him. And when she had weaned him, she took him up with her, with three bullocks, and one ephah of flour, and a bottle of wine, and brought him unto the house of the LORD in Shiloh: and the child *was* young. And they slew a bullock, and brought the child to Eli. And she said, Oh my lord, *as* thy soul liveth, my lord, I *am* the woman that stood by thee here, praying unto the LORD. For this child I prayed; and the LORD hath given me my petition which I asked of him: Therefore also I have lent him to the LORD; as long as he liveth he shall be lent to the LORD. And he worshipped the LORD there.

I will never forget the day that my wife, Nancy, and I took David to college. David was our first born. We got on the college campus that morning. He went through the processing. We got him settled in his room, we got his stuff moved in, and we gave him his final instructions on how to behave at college. We gave him a hug and a kiss, and then got in the car and drove off. We were not out of sight of the dormitory and my wife just started boohooing!

113

It was an emotional experience for both of us. She cried all the way home. I tried to console her, but she realized David was gone. I'm just grateful we only took him 30 miles from home! If we had taken him 300 miles I'm not sure I could have handled it! Nancy was releasing her child. We were releasing our child. We were acknowledging the fact that he had grown up. We had to back off and that's not easy. It's a very emotional experience to send your child off to college, or off to work, or to a new place to live and not be there to pick up after them, to love them, and to encourage them.

RELEASING CHILDREN TO THE LORD

Hannah must have felt some of that too. She had prayed for a child. God had honored her prayer, and she took the child when he was of age to the temple and gave him back to the Lord. She released him. Samuel was probably 10 to 12 years of age when she took him. We know he was able to take care of himself because in 1 Samuel 2 it says he ministered to Eli and worshipped with Eli. Samuel had responsibilities.

Hannah did what every parent can do. She raised her child and prepared him to serve the Lord. She raised him to know God, to love God, and to honor God. At the proper time she let him go. She released him to that service.

Every year Hannah would make the annual visit to the temple to take a coat that she had sewn for Samuel. Can you imagine as she was sewing that coat throughout the year, weaving the cloth, and sewing the cloth? She was thinking, "I wonder how he looks. I wonder how he's doing. I wonder how much he's grown this year. I wonder if this coat is going to be the right size."

But, each year she took the garment to him. She did it to love him and to encourage him, but she had released him to the Lord.

There comes a time that as parents we have to release our children. We have to cut the cord and let them go. I think this is appropriate today since we just had graduation. A lot of our kids are going to be off to school, so how do we release them?

Release Children From The Beginning

Begin releasing your children on the day they are born. In other words, get that kid out of your house as fast as you can! You work towards that goal to make them independent. Let them stand on their own two feet. So, from the day they are born, you start the process of helping them to grow up so they can be self-sufficient. You start releasing them the day they are born.

The way you do that is you put them in the church nursery when you come to church. You do this for a lot of reasons, but primarily, by putting them in the nursery, you get them accustomed to a stranger being with them, to holding them and touching them. You get them accustomed to separation from you.

Now, I know it's wonderful to say, "Well my child just won't stay in the nursery. My child is never comfortable unless I'm there with him."

Well folks, you are doing your child a disservice to make them that dependent upon you. Put them in the nursery and walk away. Let them cry. They will not die. You let them cry, and you don't walk down the hall and peek back and look to see if they are doing alright. Maybe you wouldn't do that, but some folks do that, and they walk away disappointed that the kids are happy and having a good time. You need to get them adjusted to being away from you for a while, perhaps for an hour from time to time.

What about when your children go to bed at night and they cry because its dark and they are afraid? Do you run in there to see how they're doing? Put them to bed and let them cry themselves to sleep. You can go in and encourage them saying, "Now everything is going to be alright. I'm in the next room. Don't worry. Nothing is going to happen." But, leave them in bed, and don't get in bed with them, coddle them, or sleep with them. And, don't let them come to your bed. You let them know that they have a bedtime.

If it's real serious you can say, "Well I'll tell you what. You go to bed and at nine o'clock I'll come in and check on you and see that everything is alright." You let them learn to go to bed without you at night. That's separation, that's helping them grow up, that's releasing them.

What about when your children go to camp? They go to camp and the first night they call saying, "Mom, dad, I'm miserable. I'm so sick, I want to come home, there is nobody I know or I like here. They put me a room with a bunch of kids who are picking on me. Come get me!"

So you ask, "Well son, are you homesick?"

He replies, "No. I'm not homesick, I'm *here* sick, come get me!"

What do you do? Do you jump in the car and run and get them? Or do you say, "Well son, we're so glad you love home and you miss home. We miss you, but you go on and make some new friends. You make the best of it, and we'll be up early Saturday to get you. But, make this week your week. Make the best of it!"

And then you hang up and go to Disney World, leaving them at camp! That may sound cruel, but that's not near as cruel as them expecting you to always bail them out when they get in an unpleasant situation.

What happens when your children are in school? Your son or your daughter gets benched by the coach. Or, your daughter doesn't make the cheerleading team. Or, the kids are picking on your child, ridiculing them, or the teachers are not treating your child fairly. What do you do? Do you march over to the school and demand that everything be fixed? No. Children must learn that you aren't going to fight their battles for them. Kids must fight their own battles. My folks always said, "Son, if you get a whipping in school, then you get a whipping at home." You know that goes a long way toward teaching responsibility. It also goes a long way in training children, who avoid being specific when dad asks, "How did things go in school today?"

Release Children By Not Being Helicopter Parents

Children don't need parents to be helicopter parents. Helicopter parents hover over their kids all day. They are ready to go down and rescue him the first time somebody looks at him wrong, or picks on him. No, don't be a helicopter parent. Send your child off; let him stand on his own two feet.

Now there are extreme cases. There are times when children are treated unjustly and a father may need to step in, but that is in extreme cases. That's the exception to the rule. For the most part, you let children fight their own battles. You let them struggle and you let them fail, because they *are* going to fail out there in life. However, you release them, so that when they do get to the age of going off to college they are able to stand on their own two feet. This is important so they are able to make it in a hostile world, in a cruel world, in a world that's unfair and unjust.

When children have parents that pamper them, hover over them, and make sure that nobody ever mistreats them, all of sudden they feel like they are thrown out to the wolves when they leave home. They are like lambs led to the slaughter, and they don't know how to adjust, so they will come home broken.

Start when they are children, when they're babies. Separate them from you, even though it may be difficult.

Do you know how a mother bear handles her little cubs? She makes them climb a tree, and while they are in the tree she stays around the bottom of the tree. When they try to climb down, she makes them go back up in the tree. When they try to climb down again, she forces them back up in the tree. After they've done that a few times, the cubs settle down. Then, the mother bear goes off and leaves them and never comes back again. Night comes and goes. The next day comes and these little cub bears are still in the tree. Finally they climb down and look around and mom is not there. Dad is not there, and they are on their own to make it.

Now that is cruel. I don't want you to chase your children up a tree and then run off and leave them. Don't move and forget to tell your children where you moved. I'm not suggesting that. I am suggesting that you help them break from being tied to you, so that they are not so dependent. Do this so that your children can be independent later on.

Release Children By Teaching Them To Release Possessions

Teach your children to be realistic about possessions. Life does not consist of the abundance of things we have. Life doesn't consist of how much we have or in what we have. We need to teach our children about materialism, possessions. Let's just think about that for a moment.

If you could make a list of things that you would like to have, think of a list.

- I'd like to have a million dollars in a savings account.
- I'd like to have a new Jaguar.
- I'd like to have a vacation home in Florida.
- I'd like to have a vacation trip to Europe.
- I'd like to have a new house.
- I'd like to have a new wardrobe of clothes.
- I'd like to have a reserved parking place right in front of the church.

Five years from now, if you are extremely wealthy and don't want very much, you may have 25% of what you put on your wish list. Most likely you will only achieve about 10% of what you put on your wish list. That's all you are going to have... about 10% of what you would like to have or want.

But now, let's go back to our children. They want a lot of things. They make their wish lists too.

- I want toys.
- I want electronic games.
- I want a motorbike.
- I want a boat.
- I want a car.
- I want designer clothes.

A survey shows that our young people get at least 75% of the things they want, either by demanding, manipulating, or whining. They get 75% of the things they desire and want; not what they need, but 75% of the things they want.

When we do this, what have we done? We have ill-equipped them for life. They will leave home and they will expect to get 75% of what they want out there in the world. Most likely they are only going to get 10 or 20%, and they are going to be miserable all their lives because you didn't prepare them to realize that they cannot have all they want.

I know one thing you're not going to get; you are not going to get a reserved parking place near the church. You can already mark that down. That's just the way it is, but we can wish for it. You don't get all the things you want in life, and children need to be taught that early on.

We are living in a false economy here in this area. Kids don't realize how the rest of the world lives. They've been taught to expect a high standard of living. You've done a great job sharing your standard of living with your children. But, I'm afraid we have been miserable failures in equipping our children with the skills they need to obtain that same standard of living for themselves. Consequently, they are not able to adjust.

Folks, somehow we have to get across to our children that they don't have to wear designer clothes. Say to your children, "Alright. You want these jeans? The generic brand of jeans is $35. The designer jeans are $60. I tell you what I'll do; I'll give you $35 because that's what it would cost to get a good pair of jeans. If you want the designer jeans, then you do some work. You cut grass, you run errands, you take the money you've saved, the money that grandmother has given you for Christmas, and you pay the other $25 or $30 that it takes to get the jeans."

In other words, let children understand that you are not going to give them the best all the time. They say, "I want tennis shoes that cost $180." Isn't that ridiculous for a parent to pay that much money for tennis shoes? So what do you say to your child?

You say, "$180 shoes? You gotta be kidding! I'll tell you what I'll do. I'll buy one shoe and you buy the other shoe."

Let them think about it, mull it over and see if they want to make the sacrifice to buy the other shoe. Let them be involved in the sacrifice. Let them give up something. You can have this or that, but you can't have both. Teach them the realism about possessions, so that they can adjust in the world.

Release Children By Teaching Them To Embrace Work

Teach your children responsibility about work. What if I were to ask you to hold up your hand if you had chores to do when you were growing up? Did you have chores for which you got no pay? Those chores were part of being in the family. There were certain responsibilities you had, and you did those things as a member of the family. You had some responsibilities. What if I asked, "Are you teaching your children to do chores for which they get no pay?" Most of those hands would come down.

We had chores, but we don't require that of our children; and that is a mistake. Children need to understand what it is to work. When they are little, they want to be helpful and it takes more time, but let your little girl set the table anyway. To start out, just let her put the napkins around or put the silverware out. Later on let her put the plates out. You might lose a plate or two, but so what?! The child's lesson is more important than the plate anyway. We all get hung up on things. Help them understand. Yes, you can do it faster and better, but don't.

Let the children bring their own clothes to the laundry room. Let them clean up their own room and pick up their own clothes. Let them help you change the linens. Show your boys how to vacuum and let them vacuum the house.

My son vacuums the house. I can say he does it better than me! And I'm grateful for that. He learned at home. Give children some responsibility. Let them cut the grass or wash the cars. Give them chores to do for which they do not get paid. Children must know that they are contributing members of the family, and they ought to contribute to the welfare of the family. Let them understand that. Let them understand that they contribute to make the family a better family.

The teenager might say, "My friends' mom and dad don't make them wash the car or cut the grass. Their parents don't make them do it."

And you say, "Oh, well. I'm sure sorry. Their parents must not love them as much as I love you."

And that's true. Parents, who do not teach their children responsibility of work, do not love their children as much as those who do teach their children to work. They do not love their children as much if they do not teach them to be responsible. In life we have to work. All through life there is responsibility, and we've lost this aspect of child rearing in America. That is one reason why we've got so many problems today. Children have no sense of responsibility to the family, no experience of work, and they grumble when they have to take out the garbage. That ought to be a child's responsibility from the start.

I have a little neighbor boy. He's not so little anymore. One day he knocked on my door. He said, "Can I cut your grass this summer?" He was about 10 years old. I looked down at the little bitty fellow and I said, "Well, do you think you can do it?"

"Yes, I can do it."

I asked, "You got a lawnmower?"

He says proudly, "Yea, I've got a lawnmower."

I asked, "How much do you charge?"

He replied, "$12."

And I thought, "Man, what a bargain!" I said, "Well you know, that sounds pretty good. I kinda like to cut my own grass, but I think I will hire you this summer for $12."

I felt really guilty about that; it was like I was taking advantage of a 10 year old. He purchased his own gas and his own mower. I talked to his parents and said, "Now, he's not charging enough and I need to pay him more."

They said, "Don't you dare. He's not cutting the grass for money. He's cutting the grass to understand the responsibility of work. We're raising a boy."

I liked that idea. I slipped him a dollar every now and then as a bonus when he did a good job, but I only gave him $12 to cut my grass.

The next year he knocked on my door and he said, "Can I cut your grass?"

I asked, "Mike, how much you going to charge?"

He said "$14!"

He went up $2 on me, and I said, "Well, alright that would be fine." So he cut the grass; the same size yard. He cut the grass when the grass didn't grow. He cut it every week, but he still only got his $14.

So the next year, he came and knocked on my door and said, "Can I cut your grass this summer?"

And I said, "Well Mike, how much is it this year?"

He replied, "$16."

I agreed. You know… I'm paying him $20 a week now. Can you believe that? $20 to cut the same yard I had, which he was cutting for $12. But he is older now, he is more responsible, he does a little better job. He cleans up a little more after he gets done.

What I'm saying is that Mike's parents are parents who said, "Michael, if you need extra money, you will earn it. You will find a job." And they set what he would charge so that nobody would spoil him into thinking he could make a lot for nothing or for a little bit of work. When Mike was 10, they knew that people's tendency would be to give more than what the job is worth, to encourage the boy. And the parents didn't want that. I thought that was pretty good for a pilot's son, for a pilot to feel that way about it. I don't want my boy over-paid; it might go to his head!

Release Children By Teaching Reverence For God

Finally, teach your children reverence for God. That is vital: to know God, to love God, to serve God. To teach them reverence for God you must teach your son or your daughter submission to your will. This way, someday it will be easy for them to say to their Heavenly Father, "Father, not my will, but Thy will be done."

You see if they don't learn that at home, they never learn it. The school is not going to teach it to them. The media is not going to teach it to them. Their peers are not going to teach it to them. An hour or two a week at church is not going to really teach it to them.

Children learn submission to authority at home, and as parents, you must learn how to break their will without crushing their spirits. You've got to break that will without crushing the spirit. Teach them about submission. You are the authority. Someday when God impresses them to do something, they will not be rebellious against God. "Not my will Father, but Thy will be done."

Children must learn it when they are young in the home. You teach them a love for God's Word and to read God's Word. You read Bible stories to them, and put little plaques around the house for them to see. You teach them the Word of God. You bring them to Sunday school. You let them be saturated with the Word of God, so that they might hide God's Word in their heart. This way, when they get older, they won't sin against God.

You teach your children a love and respect for the church. It's a place to worship and serve God. When the church service is over, you don't leave the church grumbling that the music was too loud. You don't say, "I don't like this or that. That lady in front of me, her... hair looked horrible! It looked like she just woke up!"

You don't go along saying, "...and the preacher... I didn't think he was ever going to get done. He went on and on and on and on... I wish he could have said everything he said in half the time. If he just hadn't rambled so much...."

You know, you make comments like that as you go home and what are you saying to your children? You are saying that church is not a wonderful place to be. It's not a pleasant place to be, it's not a place you want to be. You put out negative thoughts.

When you leave, you should say, "Man, wasn't that a wonderful service?! That music was so great and uplifting. Wasn't that sermon really right on target? Boy that was great! I wish he'd preached another 30 minutes; I really liked that kind of preaching! Say positive things; you don't need to lie about it though, don't take it that far!

When it comes to releasing children, you have to start releasing them right from the beginning. There are a lot of things to do and not do as parents, and you can't just say, "I'll teach them this or that later on." God has given us great responsibilities as parents; responsibilities to teach our children in the way they should go. As parents, the best way to release our children is through love, right from the start. Love your children from the day they are born. Love them enough to teach them about responsibilities and about living for God in this world. In the end, the love it takes to release your children is the same love that leads us to embrace the ways God would have us parents to walk in.

CHAPTER 11: GRANDPARENTING YOUR CHILD

First Baptist Church, Peachtree City, Georgia
<u>June 13, 1999</u>

The true image of grandparenting has changed over the years. But, there is one thing that has not changed, and that is the importance of grandparents. They play a vital part in life of the grandchildren.

Grandparents of today might be slim, attractive, stylishly dressed, and even engaged in a career… this is very different from the image of yesterday's grandfather out on the porch rocking away. Today's grandfather is probably in his red convertible or sport car on the way to the golf course! Times have changed. Grandparents are more active today than they were a few years ago. Today's grandparents may be active in the social and business worlds, but they are still important in raising grandchildren.

Someone has written this poem about grandmothers,

"Where did the grandmother of yesterday go?
The grandma took all the kids to the show,

Who would stop by to chat before we can ask
And has tackled the laundry that spilled from the basket,

Who offered to mend and make the girls dresses,
And pitch in to help when toddlers made messes,

Who came on the run when the kids needed sitting
And brought all the story books, cooking, and knitting?

Today's grandma knows how to run a computer,
She watches the markets and buys stocks to suit her,

She dons a pink smock in the hospital's lobby
And has taken up skydiving just for a hobby,

She has gone back to college to get a degree,
Sets around town in her bright yellow zee,

Grandma is still here and there's no one to match her,
But call before eight or you simply won't catch her.[16]

There is a lot of truth in that poem. I am concerned that we, as grandparents, realize our role in our grandchildren's lives and how important it is that we make a contribution to our grandchildren. Satan has attacked our youth today. There is an all-out attack in every way. There are drugs, profanity, pornography, immorality, and Satan is trying to steal our young people.

A child's parents are the first line of defense when it comes to dealing with Satan. We need to do all we can to combat Satan as parents. But, as grandparents, we are the second line of defense! Sometimes the first line of defense breaks down or it is in need of reinforcement. As grandparents, we need to be there to strengthen that line of defense, in order to save our children or grandchildren from Satan and what he is trying to do against the children. Yes, we are important in the life of our grandchildren.

I know we live in a day where many people think that when we get old, we have nothing to contribute. We are so hung up today on attractiveness and achievements that we judge people on the basis of how much they have, how attractive they are, or what we have achieved by the time we are grandparents. As we get older, we fast lose the attractiveness. We are often less involved in the world, and are often less active. So, we lose the status of achievement too. This makes it easier to put grandparents, the old folks, on the shelf, as if they have nothing to offer and nothing to give. Sometimes churches make that mistake, and so young people make that mistake too, by not looking to older people for advice, council, leadership, and guidance.

GRANDPARENTS HAVE WISDOM

We who are older have something to offer to the young and to our grandchildren. One of the first things is that we have wisdom; this is a commodity that only comes from age. The Bible says,

---

[16] Title and Author Unknown

> ***Job 12:12*** With the ancient *is* wisdom; and in length of days understanding. With him *is* wisdom and strength, he hath counsel and understanding.

When it comes to wisdom, I am not talking about a degree from college. I am not talking about having a high IQ or acquiring book learning. I am talking about the wisdom that comes from experience, experience gained through living, through raising children of their own, through watching others raise children, through involving children in the church, through relationships, and through work. Wisdom only comes from experience. This is something grandparents have to offer to their grandchildren. A grandparent's wisdom includes the experience that comes from failure as well as success.

GRANDPARENTS HAVE TIME

There is something else grandparents have to offer, and that is time. Parents are sometimes so busy they don't have time for the children. The fathers travel and the mothers are very busy climbing the ladder of success. Parents have to deal with financial problems. They often don't have the time to devote to their children. Grandparents have time, especially when they are retired. Grandparents can sit back and give time more freely.

I say to the parents, let the grandparents have a role. Let them use their time wisely with the children. A small girl has written something about grandparents. She says,

> A grandma is a lady who has no children of her own so she likes other people's little boys and girls.
>
> A grandfather is a man-grandmother. He goes for walks with boys and they talk about fishing and things like that.
>
> Grandmas don't have to do anything except be there. They're so old they shouldn't play hard. It is enough they drive us to the supermarket where the pretend-horse is and have lots of money ready.
>
> Or if they take us for walks, they should slow down past things like pretty leaves and caterpillars and they should never say, "Hurry up!"

Usually they are fat, but not too fat. They wear glasses and funny underwear. They can take their teeth and gums off.

They don't have to be smart, only answer questions like why dogs hate cats and how come God isn't married.

They don't talk baby talk like visitors do because it is hard to understand. When they read to us they don't skip words and they don't mind if it is the same story.

Grandmas are the only grown-ups who have got time. So everybody should have a grandmother, especially if you don't have a television."[17]

Grandparents have time. That is a commodity you can give to your grandchildren. Someone said to me, "If I knew that grandchildren would be so much fun I would have had them first!" Well, I can understand that because you have time to spend with them.

We will be moving back to Nashville, Tennessee in September probably, maybe October. We are moving back to Nashville, Tennessee not because we like it better than Georgia, and not because we like Nashville better than Peachtree City. We are moving back to Nashville because we have some grandchildren there. That is the primary reason we are moving: to be close to our grandchildren. We want to put in to practice what I am trying to say here about grand-parenting your grandchildren.

We went to Nashville to look for a house, knowing this day was going to come. Our son has built a new house in a new neighborhood subdivision, and he wanted us to move into that subdivision and be nearby. He thinks it is important that grandparents be close to their grandchildren for a lot of reasons. He thinks we have something to offer, for example, wisdom and time to babysit.

We do have time on our hands, so we looked around the neighborhood where our son wanted us to live. The houses there cost more than what we wanted to pay, especially in our retirement years. We didn't want to think about a mortgage in retirement years. We didn't want to take lumps of our resources, in our older years, to buy a house just to be closer to our grandchildren.

---

[17] Author Unknown.

We looked around and decided we didn't need to live in the same neighborhood. We could go a mile away or perhaps two or three miles and find a house for much less. So, we drew a circle on a map and began to look at houses within a five mile radius of where our son and the grandchildren would be living. We returned home and mulled things over.

That night or a few nights later we got a phone call from our son. He said, "Dad, we have been talking about it and we think it is important that you live close to the grandchildren. We want our children to grow up close to their grandparents. We want them to be able to go over to your house, and we want you to be there for them. We want the influence of your generation. So, we decided that if you move into our neighborhood, we will pay the difference of what it would cost you to live somewhere else."

Now, you can't turn down an offer like that! I don't care; I mean you just cannot! No one else has ever made that offer to me!

So, I said, "Son, I will tell you what I will do, I will think about it."

And he said, "Well, dad I already picked out a house that I think you will like. Ya'll can come up and look at it. We want you to come up."

He was planning for the future. We went up and looked at it. We looked at the house and said, "This looks pretty good!" So, he bought it, moved in, and then began building his house up the street. The plan was that we would move into his house when he moved out.

I say all of this simply to say that he realizes the importance of an older generation; grandparents. We have time, we have wisdom, and we have something to share.

Let me make a few suggestions on grandparenting. These are things I say also to my wife and to myself as we go to live closer to our grandchildren, all of our grandchildren; our four grandchildren, so we can be in their lives.

SUGGESTIONS FOR GRANDPARENTS

Don't Interfere In The Discipline Of The Parent

Don't give unsolicited advice. Don't be critical. If the parents of your grandchildren spank, then that's fine. If they don't spank, then that's fine. You raised your children, and you made some mistakes. They will make their mistakes too.

Unless you have a super, super relationship with your children, don't give them copies of the pastor's sermon about how to raise children! Don't offer advice unless they ask for advice, and even then, be very cautious in what you say. Do not interfere with their discipline and how they raise their children. Not only is your child a son or daughter, but one is an in-law, and you have to take that into consideration. As parents, your children don't want to be criticized for what they are doing or not doing.

Don't ask questions that are critical. Don't make subtle hints about how they ought to do things. Don't leave little notes around. Don't buy books and underscore things, and then leave them lying around for them to read. Don't interfere with their discipline of their children, that's important.

Simply be supportive of the parents' role. You are the second line of defense, not the first line. The parents have the primary responsibility; don't take that away from them. You be supportive.

Don't bribe your grandchildren. Don't tell your grandchildren that they can come and stay at your house and you will let them stay up later than their mom and dad let them stay up. Don't undermine the parents' rules. Don't undermine their discipline. Don't bribe your grandchildren.

Be Temperate In Gift-Giving

Let me say this about gift-giving to grandchildren. The Bible says,

> ***Titus 2:2-3*** That the aged men be sober, grave, temperate, sound in faith, in charity, in patience. The aged women likewise, that *they be* in behaviour as becometh holiness, not false accusers, not given to much wine, teachers of good things;...

Temperate in drinking is important to be sure, but I think this temperance applies to other things as well. It applies to gift-giving, as well as advice-giving.

Don't be the primary source of gifts for your grandchildren. If you buy the biggest Christmas present, the biggest birthday present, or the biggest gift all the time, then you are the primary source of that child's joy, and you are robbing the parents of that joy. The parent should be the primary source of joy for the child. You can give gifts, but don't overdo it. Don't give more than your son or daughter is able to give,

128

and don't give more than your son or daughter wants to give; because they need to be the source of gifts.

Be Supportive To Parents And Grandchildren

Be supportive. I had a case some years ago of a boy, teenage boy, who was kind of rebellious. His mom and dad decided to practice tough love, and they set down rules that he had to abide by to live in their home. The boy balked at them. The grandparents thought that the parents were being too restrictive, too harsh, and they encouraged the boy to move in with them.

The boy moved out of his parents' home, and moved in with his grandparents. The grandparents provided him a car, a room and everything he needed. And, the boy only became wilder in his living. He created all kinds of problems. The grandparents disrupted that family, and to this day the boy's dad and the boy's mother do not speak or get along with the grandparents. This is because the grandparents undermined the discipline, the rules, and the planning of that family. The parents made a tough, hard, agonizing decision, and they needed the boy's grandparents to support them, encourage them, undergird them, and strengthen them. The parents needed the grandparents to fortify them, but instead the grandparents were negative and disastrous in that relationship.

The parents of your grandchildren need your support, not your criticism. They do not even need your suggestions, or your lavish gifts to the grandchildren. They just need to know you are there.

I say to you grandparents, encourage your grandchildren. That's what we need to do, we must encourage our grandchildren. Not all grandchildren are going to be the valedictorians of their class. Not all of them are going to play football, basketball, or be cheerleaders. Not all of them are going to have the first chair in the band, but they all need encouragement.

All grandchildren desire approval and encouragement from their grandparents. Write them little notes, call them on the phone, and give them a little gift, like a book or something, when they do something good; encourage them. My wife's mother was such a great encouragement to David, our first born. Nana would always send a stick of gum when she sent us a note. The gum was for David, simply to say by that stick of gum, "I love you; I'm thinking about you." That's important to a child. It is important that you do that.

When Stephen was growing up we would go watch him play soccer. I must say, if they have ever created a game more boring than soccer, I have never seen it. As a spectator, it's the most boring game I have ever been to, but I went to watch Stephen play. I stood in the cold, I stood in the rain, and I stood when it was even snowing in order to watch Stephen run up and down that field, kicking that ball.

I coached one season too! We didn't win a game, but we had a great time! I am not even sure if we ever scored, but we had a good time just kicking the ball and running.

The other day we went and watched our five year old granddaughter play soccer. It was lightly raining and I thought, "I can't believe I am here again." It wasn't the game that drew us I can assure you. It was the fact that our granddaughter was playing soccer. She was running around in circles. Any time she got close to the ball we would say, "Ooohh, Carol that's good! Wonderful Carol, you are doing so good!" She would look up to see what we were cheering about and lose the ball. I don't think her foot ever hit that ball, but she had a good time. When the game was over she asked, "Did we win?"

I said, "Sure you won!" What difference did it make who won? The kids didn't care; the point is that we were able to be encouraging. We want to do more of that.

Take time to do that, grandparents. Encourage the grandchildren. Brag on them. Tell them you are proud of them. I have been grateful for the things we have had here in Peachtree City: the baby dedications on Grandparents Day and how many grandparents changed their schedules to come and be a part of it. I realize it is difficult these days to always deal with the distance folks sometimes have between them and the grandchildren, but encourage them every chance you get.

Part of being supportive is to listen to your grandchildren. It's important to listen. Most of us are not good listeners. We want and we need to tell something about our experience, our heritage and how difficult it was for us. We want to tell how we had to walk two miles in the snow uphill both ways to school. We've all been there; we've all done that, walking barefooted in the snow to school. We had to get up out of our chair just to change the channel on the TV! It was really tough you know. You remember that and you want to tell how difficult it was when we were growing up. And, your grandchildren might listen to some of that, but you listen to them.

Have you ever asked a six year old to tell you about a movie? It takes them longer to tell about the movie than the movie was. So if you don't want to hear it, don't ask them. But, listen to their hearts; listen to what they have to say. They will talk a lot, but they need somebody to listen.

A little fella said to his grandma, "Grandma, I want 'unch."

She asked, "You want what?"

He said, "I want 'unch."

She asked again, "What did you say?"

He said, "I want 'unch."

Grandma said, "No, no, you want *lunch*."

And he said, "That's what I said, 'I want 'unch.'"

She said, "I'm not going to fix you lunch until you say it right."

He said, "Grandma, I want 'unch. Read my 'ips!"

We need to read the lips of our kids and understand them. And when a teenager starts telling you something, don't interrupt them. Don't give them advice. Listen, as a grandparent, to what they have to say. Hear them out and know their heart; listen to them.

This whole message about how to act as grandparents really deals with sharing your faith. The most important thing you can do for your grandchildren is share your faith, your love in God, your love for the church, and your love for God's Word.

> **_2 Timothy 1:3-5_** I thank God, whom I serve from *my* forefathers with pure conscience, that without ceasing I have remembrance of thee in my prayers night and day; Greatly desiring to see thee, being mindful of thy tears, that I may be filled with joy; When I call to remembrance the unfeigned faith that is in thee, which dwelt first in thy grandmother Lois, and thy mother Eunice; and I am persuaded that in thee also.

You see? It was the grandmother, who had the faith and who lived the faith. The mother picked up the faith, and Timothy continued in that faith. The faith of the grandmother lived in young Timothy.

Grandparents, don't say, "I have served my time and I am going to retire." For the sake of your grandchildren, stay busy and stay active. Pray for your grandchildren in their presence. Call them by name and let them know that you are praying for them. Say the prayers with them at night if you happen to be with them, and ask God to bless them. Talk to them casually about God, and how God is in everything, and how God will take care of them.

Read Bible stories to your grandchildren. Bring them to church with you, and let them stand beside you as the pastor reads the

Scripture. Open the Bible and read it together. Your grandchildren need to see faith lived out in you. They need to see that example of someone who loves the Lord.

Don't retire and resign from your service to the Lord, to His church, or to the Bible. Let your grandchildren see an example, so someday when they have a problem, someday when there is a crisis, someday when there is trouble in life, they will say, "You know what we need? We need what grandma and granddad had. They loved each other. They held hands occasionally. They went to church together. They worshiped together. We need what they had. They had the Lord. They had prayer. They had the Bible. They had the fellowship of the Church."

Perhaps some of you do not have grandchildren nearby. You can be the model grandparent right here in this church. There are many opportunities. You could work in the nursery! And don't say, "But I'm too old!" No, you are not!

My mother is 87 years old. She's had cancer, she's been operated on, she lives in a high-rise retirement home, and the highlight of her week is when the grandchildren come and stay... sometimes as much as eight hours! She gets on the floor and rolls around with them. She reads books to them. She takes them outside to feed the squirrels, and afterwards she doesn't do anything for the next three days! But, that day is a wonderful day for her.

It takes my mom awhile to recuperate, but that's alright. The point is that you can do some of that too. You could volunteer for the nursery. You can be a grandparent to those that are not near to their grandparents. Some of you can work in vacation Bible School. You can give a few hours to come to the church just to be around. There is no preparation needed because you have learned plenty through the years. You don't need to prepare, just be there and let the children see you. Be there to dry a tear if one falls. Be there to hold a child in your lap and to be an example and model.

Don't say, "They don't need me!" Oh yes they do need you. And you need to do it, especially if you can't do it for your own grandchildren! Do it for somebody else's grandchildren. Maybe somebody will do that for your grandchildren wherever they might be. There are a lot of children that need grandparents. Be a grandparent to the little children as they grow up; be a role model. Share your faith with your grandchildren and with other children, so that they might come to know God and serve Him.

Dr. Allen and his wife, Nancy with three of their grandchildren:
Clark Allen (in Dr. Allen's right arm), Tori Allen (front center),
Carol Allen (in Dr. Allen's left arm)

Tori Allen (top), Carol Allen (left),
Clark Allen (right), David, Jr. (front)

Chapter 11: Grandparenting Your Child

CHAPTER 12: POSTSCRIPT – OUR HOPE

We often sing the words of the hymn:

> My hope is built on nothing less
> Than Jesus' blood and righteousness;
>
> On Christ the solid Rock, I Stand;…[18]

My hope is built on nothing less, than Jesus' blood and righteousness. I have one question for you, what is your hope built on?

What is your hope built on? A lot of folks have got their hope built in the materialism of this world. Others have their hope built on their education and their training. Some have their hope built on their physical strengths and their abilities. All these things have one thing in common: they are going to fade and vanish. You see, the world is long on promises, but it is short on fulfillment. When we listen to the world, the lure of the world, then we lose out.

> *1 Peter 1:24-25a* For all flesh *is* as grass, and all the glory of man as the flower of grass. The grass withereth, and the flower thereof falleth away: But the word of the Lord endureth for ever.

The glory of the world; all the glory of the world; all the world has to offer is like the flowers and grass of the field. The grass will wither, the flowers will wilt, die and fall off, but the Word of God stands forever.

Where's your hope? Is it in the world, the glory of the world? Or, is it on the Word of God? I wonder where we put our hope.

---

[18] Here Dr. Allen quotes a few lines from the song, *The Solid Rock*, Words by Edward Mote (1797-1874), Music by William B. Bradbury (1816-1868). *The Solid Rock* can be found in The Baptist Hymnal, Convention Press, Nashville, Tennessee, 1991.

> **1 Peter 1:3** Blessed *be* the God and Father of our Lord Jesus Christ, which according to his abundant mercy hath begotten us again unto a lively hope....

God says He has given us a living hope, not in the world, not in materialism, not in what the world has to offer, but a living hope through the resurrection of Jesus Christ from the dead. He leads to an inheritance that will never perish, spoil or fade. The glory of this world will fade, like the grass and like the flower; it will wilt and die.

Look at how Peter continues...

> **1 Peter 1:3-4** Blessed *be* the God and Father of our Lord Jesus Christ, which according to his abundant mercy hath begotten us again unto a lively hope by the resurrection of Jesus Christ from the dead, To an inheritance incorruptible, and undefiled, and that fadeth not away, reserved in heaven for you.

I want my hope in Jesus Christ. It's something that's eternal, something that is lasting. I do not hope in the things that will perish and fade away, or in the things I'm leaving, but the thing I am going to. I'm going to my hope someday.

A final thought from Stephen Allen:

My hope is that the words in this book have been an encouragement to each of you. My father dedicated his entire life to helping others and he based his advice on solid Biblical teaching. My hope is that you have accepted Jesus as your Savior, repented of your sins, and will one day get to the chance to hang out with me and my dad as we worship our heavenly Father.

ABOUT THE AUTHOR

1933 – Born in a field on a sharecropper's property – the nearest town was Humboldt, Tennessee, 15 miles away

1944 – Ambassador for Christ

1949 – Played football and was in the National Guard

1950 – Ordained at First Baptist Church, Cairo, Illinois. Harold Allen was a Junior in High School

1951 – First church was in Cache, Illinois

1952 – Was actively serving in the National Guard; he was the president of his class; he finished High School by correspondence and received a 10-day pass from the National Guard to graduate with his class; began "Youth for Christ" classes while he was serving in Germany

1953 – Met his wife-to-be, Nancy Clark, in Germany, while he was serving in Pirmasens, Germany

1957 – Harold and Nancy won the Intramural Debate Championship at Southern University of Illinois and were married

1960 – Seminary student and Pastor of a church in Edwardsville, Indiana

1961 – Graduated from Seminary; Pastor of First Baptist Church, Zeigler, Illinois

1962 – First son, David, was born

1965 – Second son, Stephen was born; Pastor of Twelfth Street Baptist Church, Paducah, Kentucky

1968 – Pastor of First Baptist Church, Gallatin, Tennessee

1986 – Pastor of First Baptist Church, Peachtree City, Georgia

1988 – Became a grandparent

1999 – Retired from full-time Pastor; currently serves as an Interim Pastor for churches in need

1949 – Harold Allen